PRESENTS

We are the Tokyo media team for "...yes! - Japan Ramen Magazine." This guidebook consists of select ramen shops chosen from all of the information on ramen introduced by us on our website and social networking services, for which we have conducted newly updated reports. We thank you very much for purchasing this book.

We have our special reasons for establishing this media format. While existing guidebooks also report on ramen shops as well, they feature only tiny photos and are written in very small type. And this was always something that failed to satisfy us. That's because these reports would never list the information that we really wanted to know - what the atmosphere in the shop was like, the specifications of the ramen, etc.

We truly love this phcnomenon called ramen culture. And so, in order to spread better and more detailed information, we decided to operate our own website and social networking services, and that is how we came to produce this guidebook.

As you can see from the content, our page layouts and design are distinctly different from other such guidebooks. We introduce info on the types of noodles, the sauces used in the soup, as well as the richness and strength, etc., and we feature a great number of photographs and specific reports covering even the most finely detailed information.

So then, we hope that you will discover a ramen to tantalize and inspire all of your five senses!

# Contents

Enjoy

# ramen!!

# Menya Fujishiro
## Meguro Shop

麺屋 藤しろ 目黒店

The owner, a French and Italian cuisine chef, after training at a famous ramen establishment, opened his own ramen shop in Meguro-ku. The bowls of ramen here, perfected through highly cultivated skills and a dedication to detail, are of the highest quality-from the soup, to the toppings, and to every single ingredient involved. Currently the toast of ramen freaks everywhere, you won't be able to take your eyes off this shop.

## Chicken Paitan Ramen
## with Marinated Egg

鶏白湯味玉ラーメン

### 850JPY

A chicken-based soup slowly stewed and simmered for 8 hours. A deep and rich flavor, featuring not only chicken umami and vegetable umami, but also the roasted flavor of beef and flavoring oil.

#### Noodles data

Noodle thickness: Thin
Noodle shape: Straight

#### Soup data

Rich☆★☆☆☆Light

Sauce: Soy sauce
Oil: Flavoring oil
Type: Chicken paitan

When you've finished your noodles, try adding "soup-wari"(soup thinner) to the remaining soup. You'll realize in a new way how good and flavorful this soup is.

# Chicken Paitan Dipping Noodles with Marinated Egg

鶏白湯味玉つけめん

## 870JPY

The seasoning sauce is finished a bit more sour-sweetly than ramen soup. The noodles have an enjoyably soft and chewy texture, and pair well with the soup. We hope you will enjoy the integrated tastefulness of this pairing of soup and noodles.

### Noodles data

Noodle thickness: Thick
Noodle shape: Straight

### Soup data

Rich☆★☆☆☆Light

- - - - - - - - - - - - - - - - - - - - - - - - - - - - - - - -

Sauce: Soy sauce
Oil: Flavoring oil
Type: Chicken paitan

# Menu

Menu items are listed in order starting with ramen, then Dipping noodles. The 3rd section to halfway through the 5th section is the toppings menu. After that are the drinks.

1. Chicken Paitan Ramen with Marinated Egg 850JPY ★
2. Chicken Paitan Ramen 750JPY
3. Chicken Paitan Special Ramen 980JPY
4. Large Serving (amount of noodles) 100JPY
5. Chicken Paitan Dipping Noodles with Marinated Egg 870JPY ★
6. Chicken Paitan Dipping Noodles 770JPY
7. Chicken Paitan Special Dipping Noodles 980JPY
8. Super Serving (amount of noodles) ※ Dipping Noodles only 200JPY
9. Charsiu Twice-Boiled at Low Heat Topping 200JPY
10. Green Onions (mixed with Kujo scallions) Topping 100JPY

11. Dried seaweed Topping 100JPY
12. Stewed Bamboo Shoots Topping 100JPY
13. Half Rice 50JPY
14. Rice 100JPY
15. Crispy Scorched Rice in Soup 200JPY
16. Mini Salad/Special Dressing 100JPY
17. Marinated Egg Topping 100JPY
18. Sapporo Beer (Small bottle) 400JPY
19. Black Oolong Tea 300JPY
20. Oolong Tea 100JPY
21. Change
22. Receipt

★=Recommen items

# Order & Payment

01  At the front of the entrance is a ticket machine, where you insert money and press the buttons for your chosen items

02  Sit at an available seat, and hand your ticket to a staff member

03  Water is self-service, so pour a glass for yourself!

04  Help yourself to the pepper and shichimi(blend of seven spices) available on the counter

05  When you are finished eating, return your bowl to the counter and say, "Gochisousama"

# Inside the shop

An L-shaped counter and soft lighting provide excellent atmosphere. Customers can enjoy their meal in a calm and comfortable environment. The seasonings available on the counter-top are free to use.

Counter/11

Inside the black pots placed on the counter-tops are "ginger lemon" for adding refreshing and simple flavor, and "garlic" for drawing out more umami flavor. When added to the dipping seasoning sauce for Dipping noodles, it adds an enjoyable transformation of flavor.

Surprisingly, the noodles can be eaten on their own and are still delicious. They are prepared with the utmost care and attention to detail, from the time spent on boiling them to the process of heating their container.

Inside the soup pot is a broth with slow-cooked chicken. The secret sauce is an original recipe formulated by the owner after long periods of experimentation and trial and error.

## Shop keeper's Comment

After my experience as a French and Italian cuisine chef, I became hooked on the depth and substance of ramen, and so I trained at a famous ramen place until I could open my own shop. Please come and visit, and enjoy delicious ramen, prepared with absolutely no chemical seasonings of any kind.

## Shop Information

Address:2-27-1, Kamiosaki, Shinagawa-ku, Tokyo

Open:11:00am-3:00pm, 6:00pm-10:00pm (Mon-Sun)

Open 7days

# Ramen Kaito

らーめん海人

A ramen shop that opened 12 years ago in the highly competitive Kanda shopping district. The menu offers a tantalizing lineup of diverse items including Soy sauce, miso, and tonkotsu-based soups. One of the ramen shop Kaito's distinct traits is its unusual custom of expanding its menu according to requests from customers. With its set meal menu becoming richer and diverse by the year, it offers a selection of popular items prepared with carefully chosen ingredients. This famous shop offers a menu so diverse that even regulars who come by every day can never become bored.

# Kuro (black) Ramen

黒ラーメン

## 820JPY

A distinctively black-colored soup. The sauce uses an exclusive Kaito original ingredient, a specially prepared black soy sauce. It adds an abundance of umami flavor, and is a perfect match with the tonkotsu and seafood-based soup. It's a bowl of ramen that can prove addictive, begging to be eaten over and over again.

### Noodles data

Noodle thickness: Medium thick
Noodle shape: Curly

### Soup data

Rich☆★☆☆☆Light

--------------------------------------------------
Sauce: Soy sauce
Oil: Chicken oil + back fat
Type: Tonkotsu and seafood

# Miso Ramen

味噌ラーメン

## 830JPY

The soup uses a blend of three different types of miso, with the secret added touch of hanazansho(flower of the Japanese pepper). Take a sip and enjoy the expansion of the sweetness and fragrance of miso. This ramen is overflowing with the originality of Kaito.

### Noodles data

Noodle thickness: Medium thick
Noodle shape: Curly

### Soup data

Rich☆★☆☆☆Light

--------------------------------------------------

Sauce: Miso
Oil: Chicken oil + back fat
Type: Tonkotsu

# Menu

A menu filled with abundant offerings of not only ramen, but set meal dishes as well.

| | | |
|---|---|---|
| 醤油ラーメン | 720円 | 1 |
| 塩ラーメン | 720円 | 2 |
| 黒ラーメン（豚骨魚介醤油） | 820円 | 3 |
| 麺量多 黒ぶと | 870円 | 4 |
| バトルラーメン（豚骨醤油） | 800円 | 5 |
| 麺量多 太麺醤油 | 830円 | 6 |
| 麺量多 太麺厚塩（塩豚骨） | 830円 | 7 |
| 味噌ラーメン | 830円 | 8 |
| 辛みそラーメン | 850円 | 9 |
| | 830円 | |
| しばらくお休み致します | 830円 | |
| 鶏からそば（唐揚げ3個付） | 870円 | 10 |
| 肉そば | 850円 | 11 |
| 販売終了しております | 800円 | |
| 中盛り | 900円 | |
| 大盛り | 1000円 | |
| 特盛り | 1100円 | |
| 肉盛りつけ麺 | 850円 | 12 |
| 中盛り | 950円 | 13 |
| 大盛り | 1050円 | 14 |
| 特盛り | 1150円 | 15 |

### トッピング

| | | |
|---|---|---|
| 味つけ玉子・ゆで卵 | 100円 | 16 |
| メンマ | 100円 | 17 |
| 海苔（3枚） | 100円 | 18 |
| もやし | 100円 | 19 |
| コーン | 100円 | 20 |
| きくらげ | 100円 | 21 |
| ほうれん草 | 150円 | 22 |
| 茹で野菜 | 150円 | 23 |
| 揚げたて唐揚げ（1個） | 120円 | 24 |
| チャーシュー（2枚） | 200円 | 25 |
| マー油 | 30円 | 26 |
| タルタルソース | 50円 | 27 |
| マヨネーズ | 30円 | 28 |
| 油淋鶏ソース | 30円 | 29 |

### ご飯もの

| | | |
|---|---|---|
| 半ライス | 100円 | 30 |
| ライス | 200円 | 31 |
| チャーシュー丼 | 300円 | 32 |
| チャーマヨ丼 | 300円 | 33 |
| そぼろ丼 | 300円 | 34 |
| 玉子かけご飯 | 300円 | 35 |

ランチタイム
11:00〜14:00
100円

### 麺増し

| | | | |
|---|---|---|---|
| 中盛 100円増し | 36 | 太麺中盛 150円増し | 38 |
| 大盛 200円増し | 37 | 太麺大盛 200円増し | 39 |

22

| | |
|---|---|
| ① Soy Sauce Ramen 720JPY | ㉑ Kikurage mushrooms Topping 100JPY |
| ② Salt Ramen 720JPY | ㉒ Spinach Topping 150JPY |
| ③ Kuro (black) Ramen 820JPY ★ | ㉓ Boiled Vegetables Topping 150JPY |
| ④ Kuro Buto 870JPY | ㉔ Fried chicken Topping 120jJPY |
| ⑤ Battle Ramen（Tonkotsu Soy Sauce）800JPY | ㉕ Charsiu Topping 200JPY |
| ⑥ Soy Sauce Ramen（Thick Noodle）830JPY | ㉖ Ma Oil Topping 30JPY |
| ⑦ Tonkotsu Salt Ramen（Thick Noodle）830JPY | ㉗ Tartar Sauce Topping 50JPY |
| ⑧ Miso Ramen 830JPY ★ | ㉘ Mayonnaise Topping 30JPY |
| ⑨ Spicy Miso Ramen 850JPY | ㉙ Yuchinri Sauce Topping 30JPY |
| ⑩ Fried Chicken Noodles 870JPY | ㉚ Half Rice 100JPY |
| ⑪ Meat Noodles 850JPY | ㉛ Rice 200JPY |
| ⑫ Dipping Noodles with Meat Topping 850JPY | ㉜ Charsiu Rice Bowl 300JPY ※ 11:00am 〜 2:00pm → 100JPY |
| ⑬ Dipping Noodles with Meat Topping/ Medium Serving (amount of noodles) 950JPY | ㉝ Mayonnaise Charsiu Rice Bowl 300JPY ※ 11:00am 〜 2:00pm → 100JPY |
| ⑭ Dipping Noodles with Meat Topping/Large Serving (amount of noodles)1050JPY | ㉞ Minced Chicken Rice Bowl 300JPY ※ 11:00am 〜 2:00pm → 100JPY |
| ⑮ Dipping Noodles with Meat Topping/Super Serving (amount of noodles)1150JPY | ㉟ Rice with Raw Egg 300JPY ※ 11:00am 〜 2:00pm → 100JPY |
| ⑯ Marinated Egg・Boiled Egg Topping 100JPY | ㊱ Medium Serving (amount of noodles) 100JPY |
| ⑰ Menma (Fermented Bamboo Shoots) Topping 100JPY | ㊲ Large Serving (amount of noodles) 200JPY |
| ⑱ Dried seaweed Topping 100JPY | ㊳ Thick Noodles/Medium Serving 150JPY |
| ⑲ Sprout Topping 100JPY | ㊴ Thick Noodles/Large Serving 200JPY |
| ⑳ Corn Topping 100JPY | |

★=Recommen items

# Order & Payment

01  Sit at an available seat, and view the menu

02  When you've made your decision, place your order with a staff member

03  The staff member will ask whether you want a large, medium, or regular sized serving of noodles, so please place your order

04  When you've finished your meal, proceed to the register and pay your bill

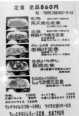

# Inside the shop

A comfortably large interior, separated between counter and table seating. Menus are posted on the walls so take your time while making your selection.

Table seat/22    Counter/6

While waiting for your meal after placing your order, feel free to read the available comic and magazines.

The ramen is prepared by highly experienced staff with great care and dedication. This is a wonderful ramen shop, continuing to satisfy the bellies of salarymen in the Kanda ward.

## Shop keeper's Comment

The first items we offered were a simply flavored soy sauce ramen and salt ramen with a chicken chintan base, but thanks to requests from our many customers, we now offer tonkotsu and seafood-based soups as well. Our set meal items prepared with carefully selected ingredients are also very popular. We are certain that you will find something to fit your particular tastes. Please come by and visit us.

## Shop Information

Address: 2-13-4, Uchikanda, Chiyoda-ku, Tokyo

Open: 11:00am-10:30pm(Mon-Fri), 11:00am-3:00am(Sat)

Closed on sundays

# Menya Inaba

麺屋 いなば

This popular shop is located near the famous tourist spot Shinjuku Gyoen National Garden, and is often busy with many foreign visitors. The owner, Mr. Futami, has experience in a variety of genres, including Japanese, Western, and French, in a career spanning 15 years. The bowl of ramen prepared here, resulting from skills cultivated from years of experience, garners a single word, "delicious."

## Special Rich Seafood
## Tonkotsu Ramen (Regular size serving)

特製濃厚魚介豚骨ラーメン 並

### 900JPY

The most popular ramen on the menu, featuring a deep and rich soup made with care and dedication, homemade ultra thick noodles, and toppings of egg and charsiu pork. A special added seasoning of citron to this deep and rich soup provides a nice accent to its flavor.

#### Noodles data

Noodle thickness: Ultra thick
Noodle shape: Straight

#### Soup data

Rich☆★☆☆☆Light

--------------------------------------------------

Sauce: Soy sauce
Oil: Chicken oil
Type: Tonkotsu seafood

# Limited Edition
# Ramen Miso Flavor (Regular size serving)

限定らーめん 味噌 並

## 750JPY

The owner's dedication to quality has led him to use the slightly sweet Jyuyonwari Shinshu Miso From Nagano Prefecture. The pairing of this miso with homemade spicy ground meat creates a splendid harmony of flavors.

### Noodles data

Noodle thickness: Ultra thick
Noodle shape: Straight

### Soup data

Rich☆★☆☆☆Light

Sauce: Miso
Oil: Chicken oil
Type: Tonkotsu seafood

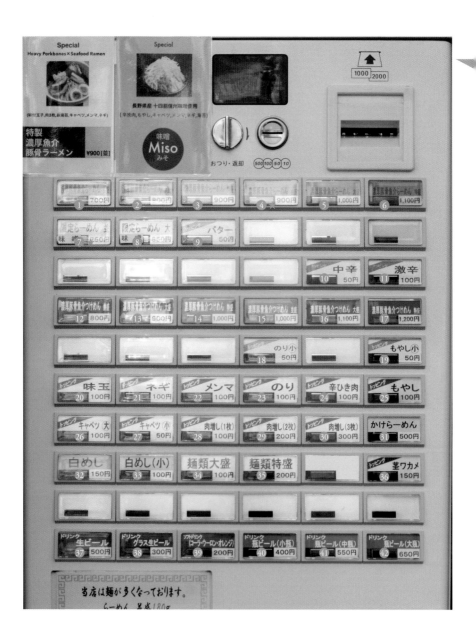

# Menu

With a large selection of toppings to choose from on the menu, you can select to suit your tastes. Please be aware that noodle serving sizes range from regular(180g), large(270g), to extra large(360g). The bottom section is exclusively a drink menu.

- ① Rich Seafood Tonkotsu Ramen/Regular size serving (amount of noodles) 700JPY
- ② Rich Seafood Tonkotsu Ramen/Large Serving (amount of noodles) 800JPY
- ③ Special Rich Seafood Tonkotsu Ramen/Super Serving (amount of noodles) 900JPY
- ④ Special Rich Seafood Tonkotsu Ramen/Regular size serving (amount of noodles) 900JPY ★
- ⑤ Special Rich Seafood Tonkotsu Ramen/Large Serving (amount of noodles) 1000JPY
- ⑥ Special Rich Seafood Tonkotsu Ramen/Super Serving (amount of noodles) 1100JPY
- ⑦ Limited Edition Ramen Miso Flavor/Regular size serving (amount of noodles)750JPY ★
- ⑧ Limited Edition Ramen Miso Flavor/Large Serving (amount of noodles) 850JPY
- ⑨ Butter Topping 50JPY
- ⑩ Medium Hot Spices 50JPY
- ⑪ Super Hot Spices 100JPY
- ⑫ Rich Seafood Tonkotsu Dipping Noodles/Regular size serving (amount of noodles) 800JPY
- ⑬ Rich Seafood Tonkotsu Dipping Noodles/Large Serving (amount of noodles) 900JPY
- ⑭ Rich Seafood Tonkotsu Dipping Noodles/Super Serving (amount of noodles) 1000JPY
- ⑮ Special Rich Seafood Tonkotsu Dipping Noodles/ Regular size serving (amount of noodles) 1000JPY
- ⑯ Special Rich Seafood Tonkotsu Dipping Noodles/ Large Serving (amount of noodles) 1100JPY
- ⑰ Special Rich Seafood Tonkotsu Dipping Noodles/ Super Serving (amount of noodles) 1200JPY
- ⑱ Dried seaweed (S) Topping 50JPY

- ⑲ Sprout（S）Topping 50JPY
- ⑳ Marinated Egg Topping 100JPY
- ㉑ Green onion Topping 100JPY
- ㉒ Menma (Fermented Bamboo Shoots) Topping 100JPY
- ㉓ Dried seaweed (M) Topping 100JPY
- ㉔ Spicy Ground Meat Topping 100JPY
- ㉕ Sprout(M) Topping 100JPY
- ㉖ Cabbage Topping(L) 100JPY
- ㉗ Cabbage Topping(S) 50JPY
- ㉘ Extra Meat Topping(S) 100JPY
- ㉙ Extra Meat Topping(M) 200JPY
- ㉚ Extra Meat Topping(L) 300JPY
- ㉛ No Toppings Ramen 500JPY
- ㉜ Rice 150JPY
- ㉝ Rice(S)100JPY
- ㉞ Large Serving (amount of noodles) 100JPY
- ㉟ Super Serving (amount of noodles) 200JPY
- ㊱ Stem seaweed Topping 150JPY
- ㊲ Draft beer 500JPY
- ㊳ A Glass of Beer 300JPY
- ㊴ Coca Cola,Oolong tea,Orange Juice 200JPY
- ㊵ Bottle Beer(S) 400JPY
- ㊶ Bottle Beer(M) 550JPY
- ㊷ Bottle Beer(L) 650JPY

★=Recommen items

# Order & Payment

01 There is a ticket machine to the left after you enter, where you insert money and press the button to choose your meal items

02 Sit at an available seat, and hand your ticket to a staff member

03 Water is self-service, so pour yourself a drink!

04 Seasonings such as fried garlic are available on the counter and free to use

營業時間
月曜〜土曜
11:00〜翌2:00
(LO・1:45)
11:00〜22:00

# Inside the shop

A distinctive interior, with a row of stuffed animals lined up in a cramped row, said to have been left there by the previous owner. The open air kitchen offers a view of the owner as he prepares your meal.

Counter/10

The kitchen, viewable from the restroom entrance. The soy sauce on the counter is soy sauce for ramen and dipping noodles. Try it if you would like to make your flavors deeper and richer.

The soup, which has been slowly simmered for over 12 hours, using over 20 different ingredients, has a deep, rich and concentrated umami flavor combining a variety of ingredients.

## Shop keeper's Comment

I have worked in a variety of genres, including Japanese, Western, and French cooking, for 15 years now. But when I became fascinated with the attraction of the deep richness of the world of ramen, I joined "Menya Inaba." I hope you will come and visit, and enjoy a bowl of ramen, prepared with the skills that I have cultivated through my many years of experience.

## Shop Information

Address:4-28-17, Yotsuya, Shinjuku-ku, Tokyo

Open:11:00am-2:00am(Mon-sat), 11:00am-10:00pm(Sun)

Open 7days

# Tsukemen Yasubee
## Shibuya Shop

つけ麺 やすべえ 渋谷店

Tsukemen Yasubee operates shops in the popular towns of Tokyo, including Shibuya, Shinjuku, and Akihabara. Every day, these popular shops will see lines of people waiting to eat ramen. The noodles here, prepared with great care to maintain their standard juicy and chewy texture, are produced in a homemade technique developed in collaboration with a long standing noodle making factory. The soup is made by simmering meat, seafood, and vegetables for 9 hours every day, and prepared through proprietary innovations so that the taste never becomes boring. Their endeavor to experiment every day, to pursue dedication to quality and detail, is probably the main reason why you will see lines forming every day at their shops.

# Recommend items

## Dipping noodles
## with Marinated egg
## (Medium size serving)

つけ麺 中盛り＋味玉

### 760JPY+100JPY

The trinity of meat, fish and vegetables form the basis of this deep and richly flavored soup which has captured the hearts and stomachs of many a diner. The homemade noodles, made with great dedication and care, use the highest quality wheat, and are a superb item, with the sweetness of wheat coming through in each and every bite.

#### Noodles data

Noodle thickness: Thick
Noodle shape: Hand-crafted

#### Soup data

Rich☆☆★☆☆Light

--------------------------------------------------

Sauce: Soy sauce
Oil: Secret
Type: Tonkotsu seafood

# Soy sauce ramen
# with Marinated egg (Regular size serving)

醤油らーめん並盛り＋味玉

## 760JPY +100JPY

A simply prepared shoyu ramen. A simple yet deeply rich, high quality bowl of ramen. The pairing of homemade noodles and a strong and rich shoyu soup is exquisite.

### Noodles data

Noodle thickness: Thick
Noodle shape: Hand-crafted

### Soup data

Rich☆☆★☆☆Light

Sauce: Soy sauce
Type: Tonkotsu seafood

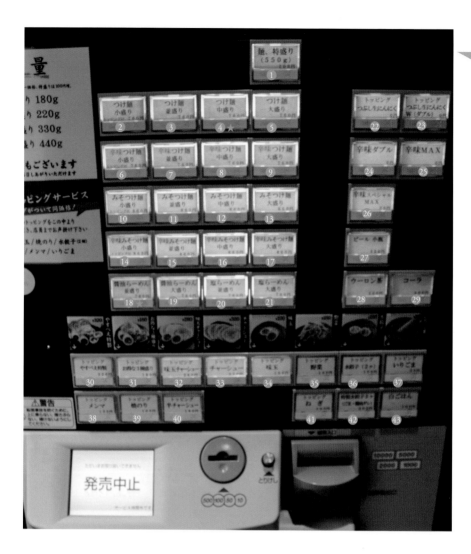

# Menu

Choose a noodle serving size! Small: 180g; Regular: 220g; Medium: 330g; Large:440g; but the price is still the same. With a large selection of toppings available, you can custom order a bowl of ramen to your tastes.

1. Super Serving (amount of noodles) 100JPY
2. Dipping noodles/Small Serving (amount of noodles) 760JPY
3. Dipping noodles/Regular size serving (amount of noodles) 760JPY
4. Dipping noodles/Medium Serving (amount of noodles) 760JPY ★
5. Dipping noodles/Large Serving (amount of noodles) 760JPY
6. Spicy Dipping noodles/Small Serving (amount of noodles) 760JPY
7. Spicy Dipping noodles/Regular size serving (amount of noodles) 760JPY
8. Spicy Dipping noodles/Medium Serving (amount of noodles) 760JPY
9. Spicy Dipping noodles/Large Serving (amount of noodles) 760JPY
10. Miso Dipping noodles/Small Serving (amount of noodles) 860JPY
11. Miso Dipping noodles/Regular size serving (amount of noodles) 860JPY
12. Miso Dipping noodles/Medium Serving (amount of noodles) 860JPY
13. Miso Dipping noodles/Large Serving (amount of noodles) 860JPY
14. Spicy Miso Dipping noodles/Small Serving (amount of noodles)860JPY
15. Spicy Miso Dipping noodles/Regular size serving (amount of noodles)860JPY
16. Spicy Miso Dipping noodles/Medium Serving (amount of noodles) 860JPY
17. Spicy Miso Dipping noodles/Large Serving (amount of noodles) 860JPY
18. Soy sauce ramen/Regular size serving (amount of noodles)760JPY ★
19. Soy sauce ramen/Large Serving (amount of noodles) 760JPY
20. Salt Ramen/Regular size serving (amount of noodles)760JPY
21. Salt Ramen/Large Serving (amount of noodles) 760JPY
22. Raw garlic Topping Free
23. Raw garlic Topping Double Free
24. Spicy Spices Double Free
25. Spicy Spices MAX Free
26. Specialty Spicy Spices MAX Free
27. Bottle Beer 350JPY
28. Oolong Tea 200JPY
29. Coca Cola 200JPY
30. Yasubee Special Topping 320JPY
31. Value Triple Sampler Topping 180JPY
32. Marinated Egg+Charsiu Topping 280JPY
33. Charsiu Topping 320JPY
34. Marinated Egg Topping 100JPY
35. Vegetables Topping 150JPY
36. Boiled Gyoza Topping 150JPY
37. Roasted Sesame Seeds Topping 50JPY
38. Menma (Fermented Bamboo Shoots) Topping 150JPY
39. Dried seaweed Topping 100JPY
40. Half Charsiu Topping 180JPY
41. Green Onion Topping 100JPY
42. Specialty Boiled Gyoza 200JPY
43. Rice 100JPY

★=Recommen items

# Order & Payment

01 Upon entering is a ticket machine, where you insert money and press the button to choose your meal items

02 Hand your ticket to a staff member, who will sit you at an available seat

03 The Dipping noodles is normally served cold(called "hiyamori"), but if you desire warm noodles, tell the staff member that you would like "atsumori."

04 Water is provided via self-service

05 The onions, dried bonito shavings, and vinegar available on the counter are free for you to use!

# Inside the shop

The Shibuya shop is always filled with customers every day. As it gets crowded at lunch, you might want to avoid lunchtime hours.

Counter/15

On the counter are onions, dried bonito shavings, and vinegar, available for free. A recommended eating style is to put onions in the soup, while sprinkling the dried bonito shavings into the soup and onto the noodles can be delicious as well. Adding vinegar to the soup can change the flavor to a more refreshing and simple taste.

Tsukemen noodles are generally served cold as "hiyamori," by chilling freshly boiled noodles to tighten their flavor, but if you ask for "atsumori," you will be served warm noodles.

We always place great dedication and care into our ingredients, because want our customers to enjoy their meals and never become bored with our food. We are proud of our homemade noodles, and our soup, for which we spend 9 hours every day preparing. We endeavor to to continue preparing flavors that will always delight, and never bore, by continuing to develop and innovate in our own unique way.

## Shop Information

Address: 3-18-7, Shibuya, Shibuya-ku, Tokyo

Open:11:00am-3:00am(Mon-Sat), 11:00am-11:00pm(Sun)

Open 7days

# Keika Ramen
## Shinjyuku Suehiro Shop
桂花ラーメン 新宿末広店

Keika Ramen, which opened its first shop in Kumamoto Prefecture in 1955. Loved by locals, Keika Ramen is a long-standing establishment, opening a shop in Tokyo as well, and for many years has satisfied the bellies of many customers. The famous Ta Lo Men is an original item only available at this franchise. It is a bowl of ramen so popular that many people have christened it their own personal soul food.

# Ta Lo Men

太肉麺

**980JPY**

This ramen is a substantive yet simply flavored tonkotsu paitan, with a uniquely exclusive soup featuring a mixture of original garlic oil. Toppings are a rare combination of raw cabbage and stewed pork cubes so soft they practically melt, a telling reminder of the unique character of this ramen.

## Noodles data

Noodle thickness: Medium thick
Noodle shape: Straight

## Soup data

Rich☆★☆☆☆Light

---------------------------------------------------

Sauce: Salt
Oil: Garlic oil(original garlic seasoning)
Type: Tonkotsu

# Keika Ramen

桂花拉麺

720JPY

A richly dense and simply flavored tonkotsu soup, slowly simmered at the shop, is topped with homemade charsiu pork, green onions, bamboo shoots, and wakame stems. We hope you will enjoy the satisfaction of the different textural flavors, and the umami of the soup.

## Noodles data

Noodle thickness: Medium thick
Noodle shape: Straight

## Soup data

Rich☆★☆☆☆☆Light

Sauce: Salt
Oil: Garlic oil(original garlic seasoning)
Type: Tonkotsu

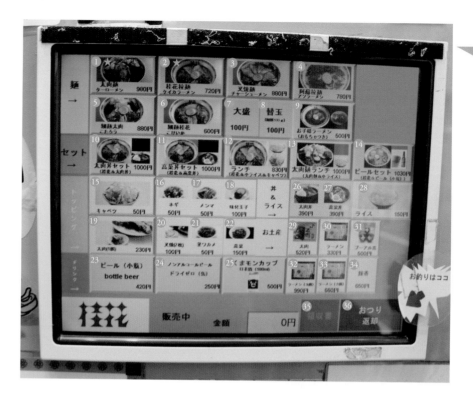

# Menu

The menu offers a wide selection, including ramen, toppings, and rice dishes. The shop also offers gift items for sale as well.

1. Ta Lo Men 980JPY ★
2. Keika Ramen 720JPY ★
3. Charsiu Ramen 880JPY
4. Aso Ramen 780JPY
5. Ta Lo Men (Small Size) 880JPY
6. Keika Ramen (Small Size) 600JPY
7. Large Serving (amount of noodles) 100JPY
8. Kaedama (Noodle Refill) 100JPY
9. Kids' Ramen with toys 500JPY
10. Ta Lo Rice Bowl Set (Keika Ramen+Ta Lo Bowl) 1000JPY
11. Pickled Mustard Leaf Rice Bowl Set (Keika Ramen+Pickled Mustard Leaf Bowl) 1000JPY
12. Lunch Set(Keika Ramen+Small Rice+Cabbage) 830JPY
13. Ta Lo Men Lunch Set(Ta Lo Men+Small Rice) 1000JPY
14. Beer Set(Keika Ramen+Bottle Beer)1030JPY
15. Cabbage Topping 50JPY
16. Green Onion Topping 50JPY
17. Menma (Fermented Bamboo Shoots) Topping 50JPY
18. Marinated Egg Topping 100JPY
19. Ta Lo Topping 230JP
20. Charsiu Topping 100JPY
21. Stem seaweed Topping 50JPY
22. Pickled Mustard Leaf Topping 150JPY
23. Bottle Beer 420JPY
24. Non-alcoholic Beer 250JPY
25. Kumamon's Sake 500JPY
26. Ta Lo Rice Bowl 390JPY
27. Pickled Mustard Leaf Rice Bowl 390JPY
28. Rice 150JPY
29. - 30. Gift Set Products

★=Recommen items

# Order & Payment

01 There is a ticket machine to the right after you enter, where you insert money and press the button to choose your meal items

02 Sit at an available seat, and hand your ticket to a staff member

03 A server will bring you water

04 Ask your staff server for refills of water

# Inside the shop

The interior exudes cleanliness, with counter and table seating. On the counter are questionnaire sheets for providing feedback.

Table seat/26    Counter/6

The ticket machine is equipped with a touch panel. There are also signs listing in detail the dedication to quality devoted towards the ingredients.

The paitan soup, a slow-simmered broth of pork and chicken bones, is milky white and refreshingly simple, without any overbearing meaty excess. The ta lo seasoned to match with the soup is succulent and juicy.

## Shop keeper's Comment

As the proprietor of the Shinjuku Suehiro shop, I have continued to make ramen for 30 years now. I continue to devote my heart and soul to preparing the soup and ta lo for Keika Ramen. The best reward I can ever receive for my hard work is when a customer tells me that our food is "delicious." On your next visit to Shinjuku, I hope you will drop by and have a meal with us.

## Shop Information

Address:3-7-2, Shinjuku, Shinjuku-ku, Tokyo

Open:11:00am-11:15pm(Mon-Thurs, Sat), 11:00am-3:30am(Fri), 11:00am-10:00pm(Sun)

Open 7days

# Hama Soba

浜そば

An abura soba shop that endeavors in the pursuit of healthy, delicious flavors. Abura soba is a type of soup-less ramen that is eaten by mixing noodles with the sauce and toppings which sit underneath. Because there is no soup, it is a healthy option that is popular with women. Because the distinct sauce uses vegetable oil, which is less likely to be absorbed into the body, the shop owner boasts that "we're the only place in the world to serve this dish!" Abura soba, a well-loved standard in Japan. We hope that all of you will get a chance to enjoy this dish as well.

# Recommend items

## Hama Soba
## (Regular size serving)

浜そば 並盛

### 650JPY

The sauce is said to be the lifeblood of abura soba. Using a secret shoyu soy sauce, a just-right level of thickness is achieved, with a delicious flavor that's not too oily. The dish is designed to firm up into the perfect balance of flavor by pouring on Chinese chili oil.

Soup data

Noodle thickness: Medium thick
Noodle shape: Curly

Soup data

Rich☆☆★☆☆Light

--------------------------------------

Sauce: Soy sauce
Oil: Vegetable

# Hama Spicy Soba
# (Regular size serving)

浜辛そば（並盛）

## 650JPY

The Hama Spicy Soba is recommended to lovers of spicy and hot food. The mixture of spicy kimchi and sauce creates an extremely good balance. This bowl of ramen provides the best matchup with the deliciously chewy medium thick noodles.

### Noodles data

Noodle thickness: Medium thick
Noodle shape: Curly

### Soup data

Rich☆☆★☆☆Light

Sauce: Soy sauce
Oil: Vegetable
Other: Spicy flavor

### How to eat Abura soba

01 Take the Chinese chili oil available on the counter to pour one circle of oil into the bowl (2 circles for a large serving, 3 circles for a W(double-sized) serving)

02 Take vinegar from the counter and pour one circle into the bowl(2 circles for a large serving, 3 circles for a W(double-sized) serving)

03 Mix well so that the sauce at the bottom of the bowl mixes with the Chinese chili oil and vinegar and noodles.

04 Eat while hot!

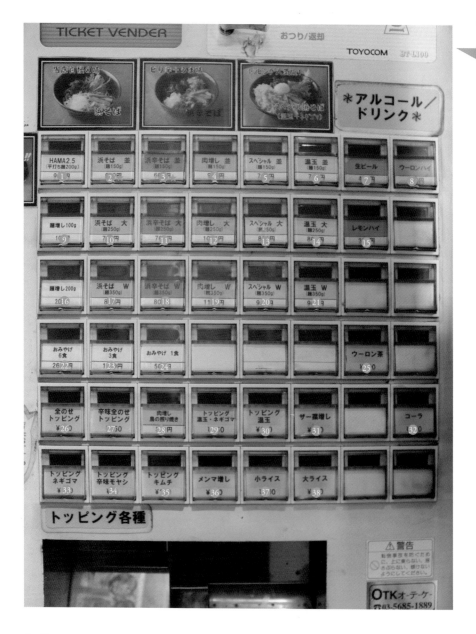

# Menu

Choose from regular, large, and W size servings of mixed soba noodles. Once you select your type of ramen, choose your noodle serving size and toppings.

1. Hama2.5(Flat noodle200g)950JPY
2. Hama Soba/Medium Serving (amount of noodles 150g) 650JPY ★
3. Hama Spicy Soba/Medium Serving(amount of noodles 150g) 650PY ★
4. Hama Soba Extra Meat/Medium Serving(amount of noodles 150g) 950JPY
5. Hama Soba Special/Medium Serving(amount of noodles 150g) 820JPY
6. Hama Soba with Marinated Egg/Medium Serving(amount of noodles 150g) 750JPY
7. Draft Beer 450JPY
8. Oolong Hai 350JPY
9. Extra Noodle(+100g) 100JPY
10. Hama Soba/Large Serving (amount of noodles 250g) 750JPY
11. Hama Spicy Soba/Large Serving (amount of noodles 250g) 750JPY
12. Hama Soba Extra Meat/Large Serving (amount of noodles 250g) 1050JPY
13. Hama Soba Special/Large Serving (amount of noodles 250g) 920JPY
14. Hama Soba with Marinated Egg/Large Serving (amount of noodles 250g) 850JPY
15. Lemon Hai 350JPY
16. Extra Meat Topping(+200g) 200JPY
17. Hama Soba Double (amount of noodles 350g) 850JPY
18. Hama Spicy Soba Double (amount of noodles 350g) 850JPY

19. Hama Soba Extra Meat Double (amount of noodles 350g) 1150JPY
20. Hama Soba Special Double (amount of noodles 350g) 1020JPY
21. Hama Soba with Marinated Egg Double (amount of noodles 350g) 950JPY
22. Gift Set Products(6set) 2600JPY
23. Gift Set Products(3set) 1400JPY
24. Gift Set Product(1set) 500JPY
25. Oolong Tea 150JPY
26. All Toppings 370JPY
27. All Spicy Toppings 370JPY
28. Teriyaki Chicken 320JPY
29. Marinated Egg·Green Onion& Sesame Topping 170JPY
30. Marinated Egg Topping 120JPY
31. Pickles Topping 120JPY
32. Coca Cola 150JPY
33. Green Onion& Sesame Topping 120JPY
34. Spicy Sprout Topping 70JPY
35. Kimchi Topping 120JPY
36. Menma (Fermented Bamboo Shoots) Topping 120JPY
37. Small Rice 100JPY
38. Large Rice 150JPY

★=Recommen items

# Order & Payment

01 At the front of the entrance is a ticket machine, where you insert money and press the button to choose your meal items

02 Sit at an available seat and a staff member will bring you water

03 Hand your ticket to the staff member

04 Adding Chinese chili oil and vinegar (available on the counter) before eating can make your ramen more delicious

# Inside the shop

You'll be greeted at the entrance by the sight of the ticket machine and counter. The walls are crammed with instructions for how to eat abura soba, and photos of menu items.

Counter/6

Introduction to souvenirs and gifts available for sale. Content of gift products are included in detail.

Using specially made noodles, requests to adjust the hardness of the noodles can be accommodated. There are a wide selection of toppings for enjoying different combinations of flavors, so have fun discovering the flavor of your own personalized bowl.

## Shop keeper's Comment

We use vegetable oil and are dedicated to preparing delicous and healthy food. Choose from 3 different serving sizes of noodles, and our expanded menu of toppings. Please come and visit, and enjoy healthy abura soba.

## Shop Information

Address:3-46-2, Yushima, Bunkyo-ku, Tokyo

Open:11:30am-12:30am(Mon-Sat), 11:30am-9:30pm(Sun)

Open 7days

# Bushikotu Taizo
## Ikebukuro Shop

節骨たいぞう 池袋本店

The soup here is superb, with a particular dedication to quality and details, using fresh ingredients fresh from the farm and prepared slowly and extensively, resulting in deliciously concentrated umami flavor. Since the shop is open until 5 in the morning, you can drop by for a bowl of ramen after a night on the town in Tokyo… with that kind of available versatility, this famous shop is brimming with such user friendliness.

# Recommend items

## Bushikotu Rich and Heavy Taizo Ramen

節骨こってりだいぞうらーめん

### 790JPY

Using a base of pork and chicken bones, along with dried bonito, niboshi, kombu and seafood umami in a blend to form this double soup, the resulting taste has a richness and substance that is just right, plus a good seafood kick, but a refreshingly clean aftertaste. Pairs well with medium thick noodles.

### Noodles data

Noodle thickness: Medium thick
Noodle shape: Straight

### Soup data

Rich ☆★☆☆☆ Light

------------------------------------------------

Sauce: Soy sauce
Oil: Back fat
Type: Tonkotsu seafood

# Taiwan Mixed Soba with rice（Large size serving）

台湾まぜそば 大盛り（追い飯付）

### 890JPY

The sauce for mixing with the noodles is a blend of three ingredients - tonkotsu and chicken bones(meat) and seafood. The meat is a juicy minced meat seasoned with snappy hot seasonings. We recommend finishing off by pouring the rice into the bowl and enjoying it risotto-style.

#### Noodles data

Noodle thickness: Medium thick
Noodle shape: Straight

#### Soup data

Rich☆☆★☆☆Light

# Menu

With a large selection of toppings on the menu, you can order a ramen customized to your tastes.

① Bushikotu Rich and Heavy Taizo Ramen 790JPY ★

② Bushikotu Rich and Heavy Taizo Ramen with Marinated Egg 790JPY

③ Bushikotu Rich and Heavy Taizo  Charsiu Ramen 990JPY

④ Bushikotu Taizo Ramen    690JPY

⑤ Bushikotu Special Rich Taizo Ramen 890JPY

⑥ Bushikotu Special Rich Taizo Ramen with Marinated Egg 890JPY

⑦ Bushikotu Special Rich Charsiu Taizo Ramen 1090JPY

⑧ Bushikotu Special Rich Ramen 790JPY

⑨ Bushikotu Dipping Noodles with Marinated Egg 890JPY

⑩ Bushikotu Dipping Noodles 790JPY

⑪ Super Serving (amount of noodles) ※ Dipping Noodles Only 100JPY

⑫ Gyoza+Rice Set 290JPY

⑬ Draft Beer 490JPY

⑭ Chuhai (Shochu High-Ball) with Lemon 390JPY

⑮ Black Pork Gyoza 390JPY

⑯ Taiwan Mixed Soba 890JPY ★

⑰ Bushikotu Ramen 690JPY

⑱ Bushikotu Ramen with Marinated Egg 790JPY

⑲ Bushikotu Charsiu Ramen 990JPY

⑳ Whisky Highball 390JPY

㉑ All Toppings 390JPY

㉒ Marinated Egg Topping 100JPY

㉓ Seared Charsiu Topping 120JPY

㉔ Charsiu Topping 100JPY

㉕ Kujo Green Onions Topping 100JPY

㉖ Green Onions Topping 100JPY

㉗ Menma (Fermented Bamboo Shoots) Topping 120JPY

㉘ Dried seaweed Topping 100JPY

㉙ Seared Charsiu & Mayonnaise Rice Bowl 290JPY

㉚ Seared Charsiu&Green Onions Rice Bowl 290JPY

㉛ Rice 150JPY

★=Recommen items

# Order & Payment

01  There is a ticket machine to the right after you enter, where you insert money and press the button to choose your meal items

02  Sit at an available seat, and hand your ticket to a staff member

03  You will be asked if you would like a large or regular size serving of noodles, so please indicate the size of your order

04  For Dipping noodles, in addition to the noodle serving size, you can also choose whether you would like cold or warm noodles

05  Feel free to use the raw garlic available on the counter. Season to taste!

※Here we follow the flow of the dining experience from entering the shop to placing your order. The descriptions will vary from shop to shop and will result in varying word counts.

There are detailed explanations of the dishes placed on the walls, which can serve as reference for your next visit.

# Inside the shop

The comfortable interiors feature a C-shaped counter and table seating. The design establishes a spacious environment.

Table seat/12   Counter/16

When the raw garlic available on the counter is crushed and added to Taizo's Bushikotu tonkotsu seafood soup, it adds to and enhances the delicious flavor of tonkotsu and seafood. The garlic is free of charge so please feel free to try customizing your flavor.

## Shop keeper's Comment

Located a 1 minute walk from the Ikebukuro Station North exit. Our cheerful staff will welcome customers with a smile. Our recommended dish is the "Bushikotu Rich and Heavy Taizo Ramen," which we are proud to note is a favorite of many foreign guests. We eagerly await your visit.

## Shop Information

Address:1-24-8, Nishiikebukuro, Toshima-ku, Tokyo

Open:11:00am-5:00am(Mon-Sun)

Open 7days

# Ichiran
## Harajyuku Shop

一蘭 原宿店

There are several big distinctions that separate Ichiran from other ramen shops. First of all, there are the semi-private format of the booths, designed to help diners concentrate on the flavors. The biggest distinction, however, are the seven customizable items, including richness of flavor and hardness of the noodles, to tailor your ramen to your own personal tastes. Try creating your own personalized bowl of ramen.

# Recommend items

## Classic Tonkotsu Ramen  -From the 60s-

天然とんこつラーメン

### 790JPY

<u>Noodles data</u>

Noodle thickness: Ultra fine
Noodle shape: Straight

<u>Soup data</u>

Rich☆☆★☆☆Light

※customizable to taste

- - - - - - - - - - - - - - - - - - - - - - - - - - - - - -

Sauce: Secret
Oil: Secret
Type: Tonkotsu

# Kaedama & Half Kaedama (Noodle Refill)

替玉・半替玉

## 190JPY 130JPY

Flavorful noodles made from an original blend of special flour. Those who have finished their noodles and want to eat more can order additional noodles. Being able to choose between regular and half sizes to adjust how much you eat is a plus.

# Kamadare Tonkotsu Ramen 3 serving set

## ※ Gift set products

釜だれとんこつ　3食セット　※おみやげ商品

The "Kamadare Tonkotsu" Ramen is served only at the "Tenjin Nishi-Dori shop" in Fukuoka. This product has packaged this superb item, featuring tonkotsu soup prepared with even richer and deeper flavor and substance, as a meal that can be enjoyed at home.

# Menu

Not only can you enjoy ramen and toppings, but dessert as well.

1. Ramen ＋ Half-boiled salted egg
910JPY ★

2. Ramen 790JPY

3. Half-boiled salted egg 120JPY

4. Kaedama · Half Kaedama Noodle Refill)
190JPY · 130JPY

5. Exttra sliced pork 180JPY

6. Extra Green Onion 120JPY

7. Rice 250JPY · Small Rice 200JPY

8. Kikurage mushrooms 120JPY

9. Dried seaweed 80JPY

10. Draft Beer 580JPY

11. ICHIRAN's Original Blend Tea 250JPY

12. Extra Garlic 120JPY

13. ICHIRAN's Original premium Vinegar 80JPY

14. Maccha Annin Tofu 390JPY

★=Recommen items

# Order & Payment

01 At the front of the entrance is a ticket machine, where you insert money and press the button to choose your meal items

02 View the seating chart to choose an available seat

03 When you reach your seat, an order sheet will be waiting for you, to select flavors to fit your taste

04 Hand your ticket and order sheet to a staff member

 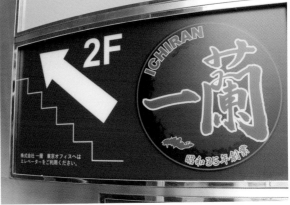

# Inside the shop

The "flavor concentration counters" were installed because of a desire to have customers deeply savor the taste of ramen. Each seat is semi-private, designed to help avoid distractions and worry about being disturbed by other customers.

Table seat/3x2室　Counter/30

If accompanied by a child, junior seats are conveniently available.

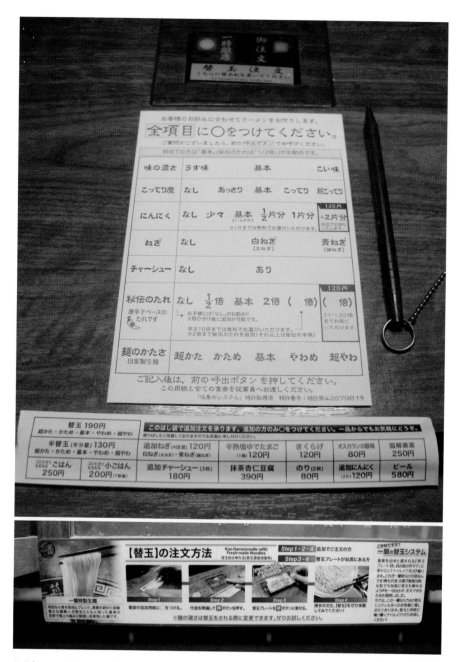

At Ichiran, each item can be selected to taste, from the strength of flavor, richness, garlic, green onions, char siu sliced pork, secret sauce, and hardness of noodles. There's no need to yell to get the attention of staff members, with a system installed by which service is available at the touch of a button.

## Shop keeper's Comment

The flavor of natural tonkotsu soup was developed by craftsmen specializing in soup during a period of experimentation spanning several years. The noodles are specially prepared Ichiran raw noodles. proudly made from a unique blend of select wheat flour by noodle craftsmen. We invite you to savor the delicious taste of ramen, prepared with special dedication.

## Shop Information

Address:6-5-6, Jingumae, Shibuya-ku, Tokyo

Open:11:00am-10:45pm(Mon-Sun)

Open 7days

# Ramen Nagi
## Shinjyu Golden Gai Annex

ラーメン凪　新宿ゴールデン街店別館

年中無休

煮干が嫌い、ご遠慮くださ

こだわりたい煮干がある

This popular shop has its own unique outlook, with its care and dedication to creating ramen, the design of their stores, and their campaigns. Transcending the framework of Japan, the ramen here enjoys great popularity overseas. The signature dish is the Niboshi Ramen, which is prepared with great and thorough care. The soup generously uses over 20 different types of niboshi(dried sardines), and lavishes over 60g per bowl. The ramen here, brimming with originality, continues to capture the fascination of many people.

# Recommend items

## Sugoi(amazing) Niboshi Ramen
すごい煮干ラーメン

### 820JPY

This soup is a totally original recipe, made through a specialized method developed through extensive research, by very experienced and trained craftsmen, and is something that no other shop could possibly copy. This bowl of ramen is the embodiment of a great deal of commitment to quality, whether in the noodles or the toppings. It is a ramen that represents the deepness and flavor of Japanese ramen.

Noodles data

Noodle thickness: Medium thick
Noodle shape: Curly, hand-crafted

Soup data

Rich☆☆★☆☆Light

Sauce: Soy sauce
Oil: Back fat
Type: Deep and rich niboshi flavor

# Additional Noodles (Noodle Refill)

追加麺

## 100JPY

Additional Noodles is a system for adding an extra serving of freshly cooked Nagi original hand-crafted medium thick noodles. The chewy texture and prominent wheat flavor fills and spreads in the mouth. The modestly curly twists of the noodles mix well with the soup.

A broad and finely thin noodle. Nagi's proprietary homemade noodle making technique results in a smooth, silky texture that is different from noodles by other shops.

The charsiu pork used here is a partially raw type, cooked at low temperatures. It tastes like a thick cut of roast beef.

# Menu

There is only one type of ramen made here, a testament to this shop's stoic style! You can sense the dedication to quality and strong convictions in their product.

| | | | |
|---|---|---|---|
| ❶ Sugoi(amazing) Niboshi Ramen 820JPY ★ | ❻ Dried seaweed Topping 100JPY |
| ❷ Additional Noodles (Second serving of thick noodles) 100JPY ★ | ❼ Smaill Rice 100JPY |
| | ❽ Rice 150JPY |
| ❸ Marinated Egg Topping 100JPY | ❾ Spicy Green Onion 150JPY |
| ❹ Charsiu Topping 200JPY | ❿ Beer 510JPY |
| ❺ Green Onion Topping 100JPY | |

★=Recommen items

# Order & Payment

01   Upon entering is a ticket machine, where you insert money and press the button to choose your meal items

02   Sit at an available seat, and hand your ticket to a staff member

03   Inform the staff member how you would like your seasonings, the hardness of your noodles, the strength of flavor, and how much "Umi no Sachi Gin Dare" (fruits of the sea silver sauce) you would like

04   Drink the water brought to you by the staff member and wait while your ramen is being prepared4

## Inside the shop

The interiors are brightly lit, with counter seating surrounding the kitchen, giving you a good sense of the Nagi world.

Counter/18

The stamp cards available on the counter offer a wide assortment of bonuses.

These soup craftsmen have examined niboshi from all of the fisheries across Japan to decide which ones to use in this soup. The amount, over 60g per bowl, is a truly astounding figure to comprehend.

## Shop keeper's Comment

In New York, we were impressed by the energy of different races and ethnicities coming together in one place, and so we decided to open up our restaurant as a proud display of our Japanese identity. We are always endeavoring to grow, with our motto, "flavor, people, the shop," serving as inspiration to this day. We hope you will get a chance to enjoy our ramen, the culmination of our dedication to quality.

## Shop Information

Address: 1-9-6, Kabukicho, Shinjuku-ku, Tokyo

Open: 24/7

# Torisoba Sanpoichi

鶏そば 三歩一

A shop specializing in tori(chicken) soba, with an absolute dedication to the quality of chicken meat. This soup is prepared using the bones, legs, and neck mainly from Abe chickens produced in Iwate Prefecture, as well as other brands of chickens. It is cooked with particular care given to its deep richness, and controlled for density. The specialists here have succeeded in producing the ultimate chicken ramen - beautiful to look at, and having brought out the absolute optimum umami flavor from chicken - a masterpiece that any discerning diner must try.

# Recommend items

# Tori Soba

鶏そば

### 730JPY

A ramen made with an elegantly simple and delicious soup, prepared with chicken stock from Iwate Prefecture chickens. A separate plate of yuzu pepper is available, and when added to the ramen, provides the enjoyment of a transformation in flavor.

### Noodles data

Noodle thickness: Medium fine
Noodle shape: Curly

### Soup data

Rich☆☆☆☆★Light

------------------------------------------------

Sauce: Salt
Oil: Secret
Type: Chicken chintan

# Tsukesoba
# (Regular size serving)

つけそば 並

## 750JPY

A deep and rich paitan soup featuring the umami flavor of vegetables added to a slowly simmered chicken soup. This is a strong and rich yet mild tasting soup. Noodles are homemade, medium thick and straight, and pair well with the soup.

### Noodles data

Noodle thickness: Medium thick
Noodle shape: Straight

### Soup data

Rich☆★☆☆☆Light
--------------------------------------------------
Sauce: Soy sauce
Oil: Secret
Type: Chicken paitan

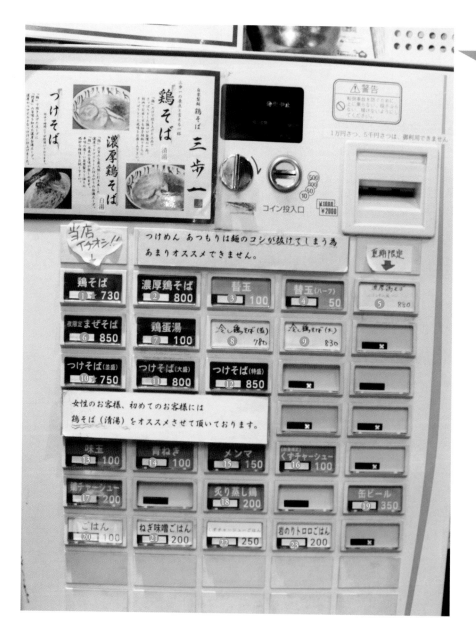

# Menu

Almost all items on the menu are chicken-based.
You can sense the confidence this shop has in its chicken.

- ❶ Tori Soba 730JPY ★
- ❷ Rich Tori Soba 800JPY
- ❸ Kaedama(Noodle Refill) 100JPY
- ❹ Kaedama/Half Saize(Noodle Refill) 50JPY
- ❺ Rich Tori Soba Tom yam kung Flavor ※ Summer limited 880JPY
- ❻ Mix Noodles ※ Night only 850JPY
- ❼ Mix Noodles Soup 100JPY
- ❽ Cold Tori Soba/Regular size serving (amount of noodles) ※ Summer limited 780JPY
- ❾ Cold Tori Soba/Large Serving (amount of noodles) ※ Summer limited 830JPY
- ❿ Tsukesoba/Regular size serving (amount of noodles) 750JPY ★
- ⓫ Tsukesoba/Large Serving (amount of noodles) 800JPY

- ⓬ Tsukesoba/Super Serving (amount of noodles) 850JPY
- ⓭ Marinated Egg Topping 100JPY
- ⓮ Scallion Topping 100JPY
- ⓯ Menma (Fermented Bamboo Shoots) Topping 150JPY
- ⓰ Limited Chasiu Scraps 100JPY
- ⓱ Chicken Chasiu 200JPY
- ⓲ Steamed Chicken 200JPY
- ⓳ Draft Beer 350JPY
- ⓴ Rice 100JPY
- ㉑ Green Onion Miso Rice Bowl 200JPY
- ㉒ Chasiu Scraps Rice Bowl 250JPY
- ㉓ Iwa Nori Rice Bowl 200JPY

★=Recommen items

# Order & Payment

01 Upon entering there is a ticket machine, where you insert money and press the button to choose your meal items

02 Sit at an available seat

03 When a staff member brings you water, hand over your ticket

04 Seasonings such as fish powder, deep friend eschalots, and homemade Chinese chili oil are available on the counter and free of charge

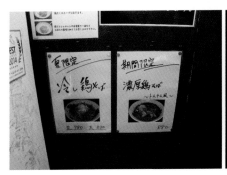

The tori soba here has a second helping of noodles available, a rarity, and also offers the choice of a half helping. Feel free to use the seasonings available on the counter.

# Inside the shop

A stylish interior that places great value on the color black.
At lunchtime the shop is overflowing with fans.

Counter/12

The homemade noodle-making area lies at the back of the shop. Because the soup is mild, in order to give the ramen some punch, the noodles are prepared with a bit of hardness to them.

## Shop keeper's Comment

When I was training at a famous ramen shop in Saitama, I became fascinated by the appeal of tori soba. Thanks to the experience I gained during my training, I have built upon that to try to prepare a bowl of ramen with the greatest dedication and care in the soup, the noodles, and toppings. We also offer a large lineup of toppings to enjoy changes and variations in flavor. These are flavors that you can eat everyday and never tire of, so I hope you will come by and dine with us.

## Shop Information

Address:2-14-9, Takadanobaba, Shinjuku-ku, Tokyo

Open: 11:00am-3:00pm, 6:00pm-11:30pm (Mon-Sun)

Open 7days

# Mensakedokoro
Burari

麺酒処ぶらり

This famous shop stands apart, like a hideaway, tucked in between buildings. The selling point of this shop is none other than its "chicken paitan." Here you can enjoy a superb ramen that has had many a ramen freak clucking with satisfaction. And on the 2nd floor is an izakaya that opens after 17:30, and is recommended as a place to enjoy ramen as a finishing touch on a night of good times.

# Recommend items

## Chicken Paitan Ramen

鶏白湯ラーメン

### 820JPY

The soup, a mixture of 3 different types of chicken bones weighing over 70 kg, with seasoned vegetables and some other special ingredients, is simmered on high heat for over 5 hours, and is a masterpiece of tightly concentrated chicken umami flavor. Beautifully matched with medium thick noodles, you will no doubt slurp this bowl down furiously to the very last drop.

#### Noodles data

Noodle thickness: Medium
Noodle shape: Flat

#### Soup data

Rich☆★☆☆☆Light

- - - - - - - - - - - - - - - - - - - - - - - - - - - - - - - - - - -

Sauce: Paitan
Oil: Chicken oil
Type: Chicken paitan

## Noodles data

Noodle thickness: Medium fine
Noodle shape: Straight

## Soup data

Rich☆★☆☆☆Light

--------------------------------------------

Sauce: Salt
Oil: Chicken oil
Type: Chicken paitan

# Chicken Paitan Dipping Noodles

鶏白湯つけめん

## 870JPY

Thick and rich chicken paitan dipping sauce is prepared with just as much care and dedication as are the noodles, in this dish separating soup from noodles. A key point of distinction is in the use of medium fine noodles that will better mix with the soup. It's a choice that emanates with powerful convictions.

# Menu

A popular topping is #13, the marinated egg. Those who want to eat extra noodles should press button #4 and order a large serving ticket.

- ❶ Chicken Paitan Ramen with Marinated Egg 930JPY
- ❷ Chicken Paitan Ramen 820JPY ★
- ❸ Spicy Chicken Paitan Ramen 840JPY
- ❹ Large Serving (amount of noodles) 120JPY
- ❺ Tori Soba with Marinated Egg 810JPY
- ❻ Tori Soba 700JPY
- ❼ Spicy Tori Soba 720JPY
- ❽ Chicken Paitan Dipping Noodles 870JPY ★
- ❾ Chicken × Seafood Dipping Noodles 870JPY

- ❿ Chicken Charsiu Topping 150JPY
- ⓫ Spicy Green Onion Topping 200JPY
- ⓬ Marinated Egg Topping 120JPY
- ⓭ Spicy Chicken Charsiu Topping 100JPY
- ⓮ Chicken Gyoza 450JPY
- ⓯ Rice with Raw Egg 200JPY
- ⓰ Rice 110JPY
- ⓱ Draft Beer 500JPY

★=Recommen items

# Order & Payment

01  Upon entering is a ticket machine, where you insert money and press the button to choose your meal items

02  Sit at an available seat

03  A staff member will bring you water, upon which you will hand over your ticket

04  Please feel free to use the seasonings on the counter!

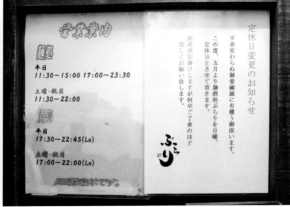

# Inside the shop

An abundance of wood furnishings and detailed attention to lighting lend a comfortable atmosphere to the interiors. This is a relaxing and calm environment.

Table seat/12    Counter/5

On the counter are pepper, soy sauce, vinegar, and other seasonings. Recommended for use with side dishes, etc.

Great care and dedication is put into the noodles/noodle choices are changed according to the recipe. One of the distinctions of the noodles used here are that the thickness and the amount of water are adjusted to pair well with each type of soup.

The main soup ingredient/Chicken paitan is slowly cooked and becomes gelatinous when left to cool in a refrigerator. Almost like cheese.

## Shop keeper's Comment

Because the shop is operated as an izakaya after 17:30, the interior features a large number of table seats. There is a second floor as well, where customers can enjoy drinks in a comfortable and relaxing space. And ordering ramen as a finishing touch after some drinks is allowed here.

## Shop Information

Address:5-52-5, Higashinippori, Arakawa-ku, Tokyo, Japan

Open:11:30am-3:00pm, 5:30pm-10:45pm (Mon-Fri), 11:30am-10:00pm(Sat), 2F: 5:30 pm～10:00pm(Sat)

Closed on Sundays

# Yarou Ramen
## Akihabara Shop

野郎ラーメン 秋葉原店

Among the many ramen shops in Akihabara, this shop boasts a reputation as being one of the very best. In any case we would like to recommend this shop to anybody who wants to eat a satisfyingly full meal. In Japan, large servings of ramen are called "gattsuri-kei"(hearty type), and this one is mega loaded with meat and vegetables. You will definitely want to pay them a visit when shopping in Akihabara.

# Recommend items

## Ajitama(Marinated egg) Yarou Ramen

味玉野郎ラーメン

### 830JPY

The deeply dense and rich soup is delicious, cooked for a long time to extract umami flavor, adding seasoned vegetables to several varieties of meat, including pork bone and chicken. With a combination of crisp vegetables and ajitama(marinated egg), together with charsiu pork, this is a mixture that ramen lovers will find irresistible.

## Noodles data

Noodle thickness: Medium thick
Noodle shape: Curly
※Photo shows medium thick curly noodles

## Soup data

Rich☆☆★☆☆Light

--------------------------------------------------

Sauce: Soy sauce
Oil: Back fat
Type: Tonkotsu

# Mega Butayarou Ramen

メガ豚野郎ラーメン

## 1000JPY

3 slices of charsiu pork - made with only the choicest pork - are extravagantly served as toppings. And not only do you get these 3 cubed pieces of pork, but also extremely thick bamboo shoots, dried seaweed, and marinated eggs. Total weight is approximately 1.5 kg, providing for a bowl of ramen that is wholly satisfying in both flavor and quantity.

### Noodles data

Noodle thickness: Medium thick
Noodle shape: Curly

※Choices available between medium thick curly noodles and ultra thick flat noodles. Photo shows medium thick curly noodles.

### Soup data

Rich☆☆★☆☆Light

Sauce: Soy sauce
Oil: Back fat
Type: Tonkotsu

# Menu

Menu recommendations offer a choice of noodle types between flat and curly.

1. Yarou Ramen 730JPY
2. Small Size Butayarou Ramen 780JPY
3. Ajitama Yarou Ramen 830JPY ★
4. Butayarou Ramen 930JPY
5. Mega Butayarou Ramen 1000JPY ★
6. Special Soupless Yarou Noodles 850JPY
7. Soupless Yarou Noodles 750JPY
8. Soupless Butayarou Noodles 950JPY
9. Miso Tama Yarou Ramen 880JPY
10. Miso Yarou Ramen 780JPY
11. Small Size Miso Butayarou Ramen 830JPY
12. Miso Cheese Yarou Ramen 950JPY
13. Miso Butayarou Ramen 980JPY
14. Miso Mega Butayarou Ramen 1050JPY
15. Stamina Tuke Yarou(Dipping Noodles) ※ Cold or Hot 850JPY
16. Stamina Tuke Yarou with Marinated Egg(Dipping Noodles) ※ Cold or Hot 950JPY
17. Stamina Tuke Butayarou(Dipping Noodles) ※ Cold or Hot 1050JPY
18. Tan Tan Yarou Noodles 880JPY
19. Soupless Tan Tan Noodles 880JPY

20. Marinated Egg Topping 100JPY
21. Roasted Vegetables Topping 100JPY
22. Spicy Tempura bits Topping 50JPY
23. Hokkaido Luxury Cheese Topping 150JPY
24. Sweet Corn Topping 100JPY
25. Dried seaweed Topping 100JPY
26. Raw Egg Topping 50JPY
27. Thick Menma (Fermented Bamboo Shoots)Topping 100JPY
28. Extra Meat Topping 200JPY
29. Boiled Gyoza 380JPY
30. Yarrow Charsiu Rice Bowl 280JPY
31. Rice 100JPY
32. Draft Beer(L) 500JPY
33. Draft Beer(S) 300JPY
34. Bottle Beer 500JPY
35. Whiskey highball 280JPY
36. Hoppy 300JPY
37. Hoppy's Shochu 100JPY
38. Coca Cola 200JPY

★=Recommen items

# Order & Payment

01 At the front of the entrance is a ticket panel, where you insert money and press the button to choose your meal items

02 Sit at an available seat and hand your ticket to a staff member

03 Your server will ask if you want free toppings, extra garlic, kaeshi(a mixture of soy sauce, sugar and mirin), to change your noodles to ultra thick, extra vegetables, etc., so you can customize to your own personal tastes.

04 Water is self-service, so pour yourself a drink!

05 On the counter are pepper, cayenne pepper powder, "punch up sauce" for thickening and deepening the flavor of ramen and gyoza, and garlic. Try them out in accordance with your preferences

Seasonings available on the counter are free, so please feel free to season your food to fit your tastes.

# Inside the shop

The 1st floor offers counter seating, with a good view of the kitchen. The 2nd floor offers table and counter seating, for a relaxed dining atmosphere.

Table seat/12    Counter/24

The staff are proficient and skilled at handling even the most detailed orders from customers. The shop original T-shirts are cool too.

## Shop keeper's Comment

I've been working as a staff member ever since the Akihabara shop opened, but lately we've enjoyed an increase in foreign customers. We are working hard to offer the most delicious ramen to fit each customer's preferences. On your next visit to Akihabara, we hope you'll drop by and eat our ramen.

## Shop Information

Address:3-2-11, Sotokanda, Chiyoda-ku, Tokyo

Open:11:00am-10:30pm(Mon-Sat), 11:00am-10:00pm(Sun)

Open 7days

# Menya Mogura

麺屋 土竜

Mogura, opened in 2014, but instantly entered the ranks of the most popular ramen shops. While the quality of their ramen is a given, they exercise great care and detail into their toppings as well. And every 29th of the month is celebrated as "Meat Day"("29" is pronounced as "niku" with "ni"=2 and "ku"=9 in Japanese) with a chunk of meat topping added as a free service. With original ideas such as topping dipping noodles with both fried and boiled vegetables, this is an up and coming shop that endeavors to create ever unique styles of ramen.

# Recommend items

## Mogura's Dipping Noodles

土竜つけ麺

### 980JPY

The biggest distinction of this dish are the vegetable toppings. With a dedication to fresh ingredients, and from a concern to help diners "enjoy the difference between texture and flavor," this shop offers preparation styles catered to the cooking method most optimal for each ingredient, whether it be boiling or frying, etc. The soup is prepared using large amounts of expensive mackerel, Murota dried bonito, and thick bonito shavings to extract a soup stock, resulting in an enjoyable fusion of savory meat-based tonkotsu and chicken stock with the extravagant flavor of seafood stock. After finishing the noodles, the soup can be diluted into a tomato and ginger soup, a novel and creative idea.

## Noodles data

Noodle thickness: Thick
Noodle shape: Straight

## Soup data

Rich☆★☆☆☆Light

---------------------------------------------------

Sauce: Soy sauce
Oil: Bonito oil
Type: Tonkotsu seafood

# Charsiu Ramen

チャーシューめん

## 1050JPY

Mogura's proudly served charsiu pork is so soft and succulent that it crumbles when picked up with chopsticks, with the surfaces broiled to an absolutely wonderfully fragrant aroma. The soup is a deep and rich tonkotsu seafood based Soy sauce flavor. And while rich and strong, has a refreshingly light aftertaste.

### Noodles data

Noodle thickness: Medium thick
Noodle shape: Straight

### Soup data

Rich☆★☆☆☆Light

------------------------------------------------

Sauce: Soy sauce
Oil: Bonito oil
Type: Tonkotsu seafood

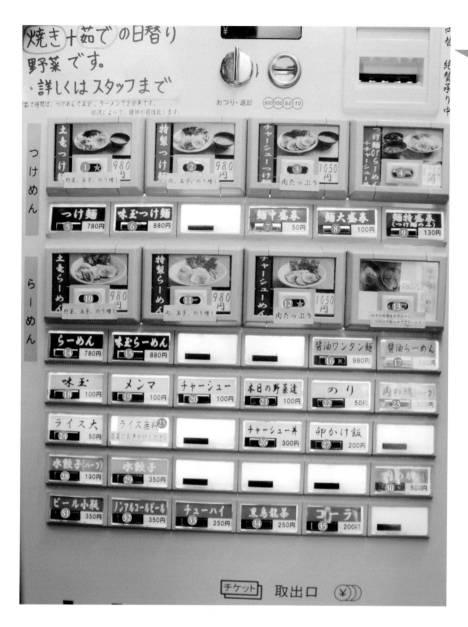

# Menu

The charsiu pork and meat chunks are very popular. We also recommend ordering their proudly served vegetables since they can be ordered separately.

| | |
|---|---|
| ❶ Mogura's Dipping Noodles 980JPY  ★ | ⓲ Marinated Egg Topping 100JPY |
| ❷ Special Dipping Noodles 980JPY | ⓳ Menma (Fermented Bamboo Shoots) Topping 100JPY |
| ❸ Charsiu Dipping Noodles 1050JPY | ⓴ Charsiu Topping 100JPY |
| ❹ Dipping Noodles or Ramen ＋ Charsiu Rice Bowl 1050JPY | ㉑ Today's vegetables Topping 100JPY |
| ❺ Dipping Noodles 780JPY | ㉒ Dried seaweed Topping 50JPY |
| ❻ Dipping Noodles with Marinated Egg    880JPY | ㉓ Meat Loaf/Half Size 300JPY |
| ❼ Medium Serving (amount of noodles) 50JPY | ㉔ Rice 50JPY |
| ❽ Large Serving (amount of noodles)100JPY | ㉕ Small Rice Free |
| ❾ Super Serving (amount of noodles) ※ Dipping Noodles Only130JPY | ㉖ Charsiu Rice Bowl 300JPY |
| ❿ Mogura's Ramen 980JPY | ㉗ Rice with Raw Egg 200JPY |
| ⓫ Special Ramen 980JPY | ㉘ Boiled Gyoza/Half Size 190JPY |
| ⓬ Charsiu Ramen 1050JPY  ★ | ㉙ Boiled Gyoza 350JPY |
| ⓭ Dipping Noodles Japanese citron flavor 780JPY | ㉚ Meat Loaf 500JPY |
| ⓮ Ramen   780JPY | ㉛ Bottle Beer 350JPY |
| ⓯ Ramen with Marinated Egg 880JPY | ㉜ Non-alcoholic beer 350JPY |
| ⓰ Soy sauce with Wanton 980JPY | ㉝ Chuhai (Shochu High-Ball) 250JPY |
| ⓱ Soy sauce Ramen 780JPY | ㉞ Black Oolong Tea 250JPY |
| | ㉟ Coca Cola 200JPY |

★=Recommen items

# Order & Payment

01  Upon entering there is a ticket machine, where you insert money and press the button to choose your meal items

02  Sit at an available seat, and a staff member will bring you water

03  Hand your ticket to the staff member

04  If you need a paper apron or a hairband please ask a staff member

133

# Inside the shop

The counter seats surround the kitchen area, so you can view the staff as they
prepare your meal.

Table seat/4    Counter/9

If you order a large or bigger serving of dipping noodles, you can get a second serving of soup. A nice and considerate touch.

By combining both fried and boiled vegetables, you can enjoy the differences in flavor of the ingredients. By broiling the charsiu before serving, they become doubly fragrant. It's fun just to watch how carefully and thoroughly the staff works.

## Shop keeper's Comment

We want to spend the time and effort in order to provide delicious food. We are always experimenting with new preparation methods and ingredients in order to provide even better and more delicious dishes, so we hope you will come by and dine with us.

## Shop Information

Address: 2-6-11, Shibadaimon, Minato-ku, Tokyo, Japan

Open: 11:00am-9:00pm (Mon-Fri), 11:00am-5:00pm (Sat)

Closed on Sundays

# Torisoba Jyuban 156
## Azabujyuban Shop

鶏蕎麦十番 156 麻布十番本店

The new and innovative style of 156 (pronounced "Ichikoro"), which has evolved from the unique Japanese format of "ramen-ya" to the modern "ramen bar." It can be said that you will not find anything else in Tokyo that comes close to the stylish atmosphere found here. Every day is in the pursuit of creating the most superb bowl of ramen, and the highly perfected ramen here is super popular. The menu is filled with a large number of side dishes as well, including takoyaki, gyoza, and chicken legs. This is the rare shop where you can comfortably settle in and enjoy a great meal.

# Recommend items

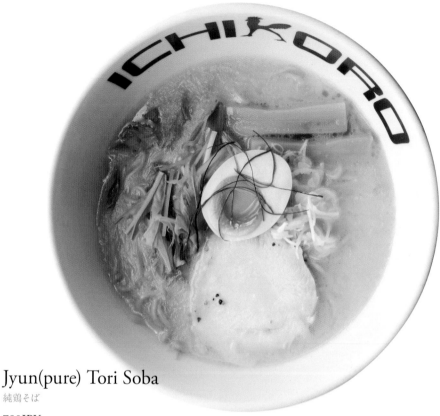

## Jyun(pure) Tori Soba

純鶏そば

### 780JPY

The soup is made using chicken bones, feet, and neck from Kyushu-produced chickens, together with vegetables, and slowly simmered for over 6 hours to create a Japanese-made chicken paitan - deep and rich with chicken umami which floods the mouth with delicious flavor. The char siu toppings are made with healthy chicken breast meat, providing a very juicy and flavorful taste.

## Noodles data

Noodle thickness: Medium fine
Noodle shape: Straight

## Soup data

Rich☆★☆☆☆Light

Sauce: Salt
Oil: Chicken oil
Type: Chicken paitan

# Spicy Shrimp Tantan-Men

## ※ without soup

エビ辛担々麺 ※汁なし

## 900JPY

The sauce is an original creation, using a Chinese chili oil made from 11 spices and 18 different ingredients. The flavor is maintained using a homemade meat miso and spices, to create a very nice balance! Happily, you can choose between warm and cold noodles.

### Noodles data

Noodle thickness: Thick
Noodle shape: Straight

### Soup data

Rich ★☆☆☆☆ Light

Sauce: Original tantan sauce
Oil: Green onion oil, shrimp oil

### Popular side menu

Takoyaki
550JPY

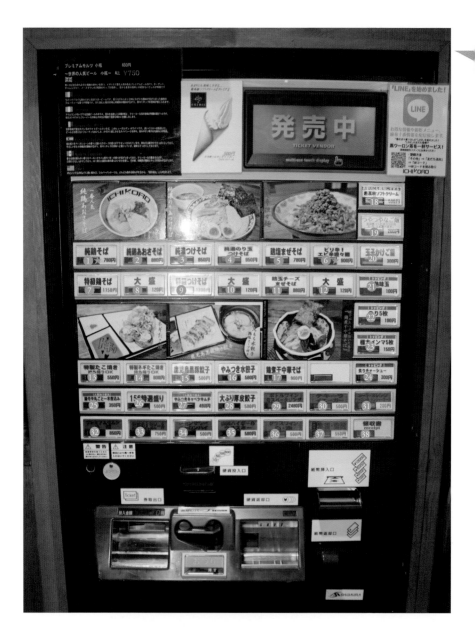

# Menu

The menu features not only ramen, but happily,
also a wide selection of side dishes and sake.

| | |
|---|---|
| ❶ Jyun Tori Soba 780JPY ★ | ⓴ Rice with Raw Egg 300JPY |
| ❷ Jyun Tori Soba with Sea Lettuce 880JPY | ㉑ Marinated Egg Topping 100JPY |
| ❸ Jyun Rich Dipping Noodles 850JPY | ㉒ Dried seaweed Topping 100JPY |
| ❹ Jyun Rich Dipping Noodles with Marinated Egg & Seaweed 950JPY | ㉓ Thick Menma (Fermented Bamboo Shoots) Topping 150JPY |
| ❺ Chicken Salt Mix Noodles 780JPY | ㉔ Broiled Charsiu Topping 300JPY |
| ❻ Spicy Shrimp Tantan-Men 900JPY ★ | ㉕ Whole Boiled Chicken 350JPY |
| ❼ Special Tori Soba 1150JPY | ㉖ 156 Specially Set 500JPY |
| ❽ Special Tori Soba/Large Serving (amount of noodles) 120JPY | ㉗ Cabbage Kimchi 480JPY |
| ❾ Special Dipping Noodles 1200JPY | ㉘ Large Thick-Skinned Gyoza 500JPY |
| ❿ Special Dipping Noodles/Large Serving (amount of noodles) 120JPY | ㉙ Bottle of Wine,Sparkling Wine 2480JPY |
| ⓫ Chicken Mix Noodles with Marinated Egg & Cheese880JPY | ㉚ Tequila,Jägermeister 500JPY |
| ⓬ Chicken Mix Noodles/Large Serving (amount of noodles) 120JPY | ㉛ Coca Cola,Orange Juice,Oolong Tea,Ginger Ale 200JPY |
| ⓭ Special Tako Yaki 600JPY | ㉜ Bottle Beer 650JPY |
| ⓮ Special Tako Yaki with Green Onion 650JPY | ㉝ World of Beer 750JPY |
| ⓯ Kagoshima's Blackpork Gyoza 500JPY | ㉞ Shochu High-Ball Lemon flavor · Oolong Hai 500JPY |
| ⓰ Boiled Gyoza 580JPY | ㉟ Whiskey highball 580JPY |
| ⓱ Chicken Chuka Soba 900JPY | ㊱ Glass of Wine/White or Red 500JPY |
| ⓲ Soft Ice Cream 500JPY | ㊲ Sake,Shochu 550JPY |
| ⓳ Rice 200JPY | ㊳ Receipt |

★ =Recommen items

# Order & Payment

01  Upon entering there is a ticket machine, where you inscrt money and press the button to choose your meal items, and receive tickets which you hand to a staff member

02  Sit at an available seat

03  Water is provided via self-service

04  Please use the Chinese chili oil, Japanese pepper, and pepper, available on the counter

# Inside the shop

The shop is brightly lit, clean and designed to feel like a bar. This is an environment where you can rest your feet when you're tired from all the sightseeing.

Table seat/8   Counter/16

A wide selection of alcoholic drinks are available, including wine, shochu, whiskey, tequila, and beers.

The chicken paitan soup uses no beef or pork, prepared using only chicken and vegetables, to create a deep and rich soup. There is also a teppan plate for making takoyaki here, something uncommon in a ramen shop.

## Shop keeper's Comment

After gaining experience at izakayas and ramen specialty shops, I have participated here at 156 since its opening. Our concept is to create an environment where even first-time customers can relax and enjoy themselves from the moment they enter to the time they leave. We offer a ramen bar style where you can enjoy drinks as well. We hope you will drop by after enjoying the day sightseeing.

## Shop Information

Address:2-1-10, Azabujuban, Minato-ku, Tokyo

Open:11:00am-4:00am(Mon-Sun)

Open 7days

# Chuka Soba
# Tanakaya

中華そば 田中屋

This shop belongs to an ultra famous chain of ramen shops called "Tanaka Shoten." The food cooked here is prepared on the concept of "gently flavored, comforting ramen," and offers delicious tastes that are brimming with originality. This shop is superb in its aesthetic sensibility and dedication to quality - for example, using celadon porcelain for their bowls because it makes their soup look beautiful.

# Recommend items

## Chuka Soba

中華そば

### 780JPY

What you need to see here is how clear the soup is! In order to get tonkotsu soup to become so clear, all of the coagulated foam needs to be carefully and painstakingly skimmed off. And of course, the flavor is outstanding. The flat noodles mix well together with the soup, and these too taste amazing.

#### Noodles data

Noodle thickness: Medium
Noodle shape: Flat

#### Soup data

Rich ☆☆☆☆★ Light

------------------------------------------------

Sauce: Salt
Oil: None
Type: Tonkotsu

# Yamagata
# aSpicy Miso Ramen

山形辛味噌らーめん

## 900JPY

A spicy miso ramen modeled after a famous ramen shop in Yamagata Prefecture. By stirring in the spicy miso - placed right in the middle of the bowl - it adds a spicy kick to the refreshingly simple soup and is very delicious. The charsiu pork toppings are so soft and succulent they'll crumble when you pick them up with your chopsticks.

### Noodles data

Noodle thickness: Medium
Noodle shape: Flat

### Soup data

Rich☆☆☆★☆Light

Sauce: Miso
Oil: Chicken oil
Type: Tonkotsu

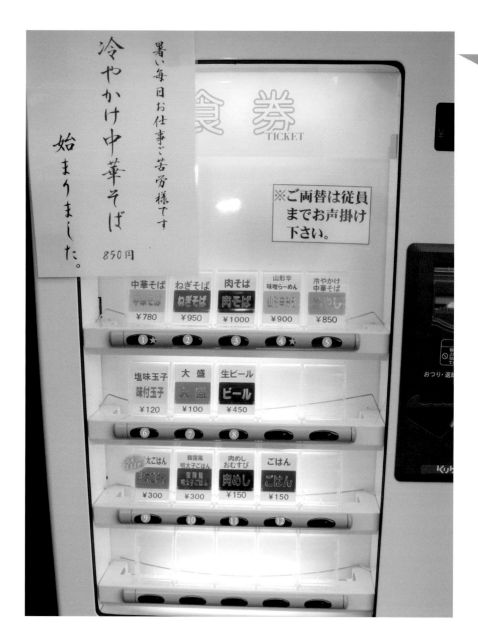

# Menu

With such a limited number of items on the menu,
you can sense the confidence they have in their product.

1. Chuka Soba 780JPY ★
2. Green Onion Soba 950JPY
3. Meat Soba 1000JPY
4. Yamagata Spicy Miso Ramen 900JPY ★
5. Cold Chuka Soba 850JPY
6. Salted Soft-Boiled Egg,Marinated Egg 120JPY
7. Large Serving (amount of noodles) 100JPY
8. Draft Beer 450JPY
9. Marinated cod roe Rice Bowl 300JPY
10. Korean-style Marinated cod roe Rice Bowl 300JPY
11. Meat Rice Bowl 150JPY
12. Rice 150JPY

★=Recommen items

# Order & Payment

01 Upon entering is a ticket machine, where you insert money and press the button to choose your meal items

02 Sit at an available seat

03 Hand your ticket to the staff member

04 Water is self-service, so pour yourself a drink!

05 Feel free to use the raw garlic and ginger available on the counter.
Please season to taste!

## Inside the shop

A stately wooden counter is designed to envelop the kitchen area. Diners who like their ramen thick and heavy can ask for back fat to be added, so please ask a staff member.

Counter/13

A side dish called meat & rice. We have a seasoning called special chinese chili, so please feel free to use it.

It takes a bit of time to boil the medium thick flat noodles.
The very juicy charsiu pork is a highlight item of Tanakaya.

"Chuka Soba Tanakaya" is a ramen shop affiliated with the "Tanaka Shoten" brand. Since opening, we have always worked hard to prepare delicious ramen. We will continue as a member of the Tanaka Shoten brand to put in our best efforts, and hope that you will come by and dine with us.

## Shop Information

Address:6-8, Kagurazaka, Shinjuku-ku, Tokyo

Open:11:00am-9:00pm(Mon-Sun)

Open 7days

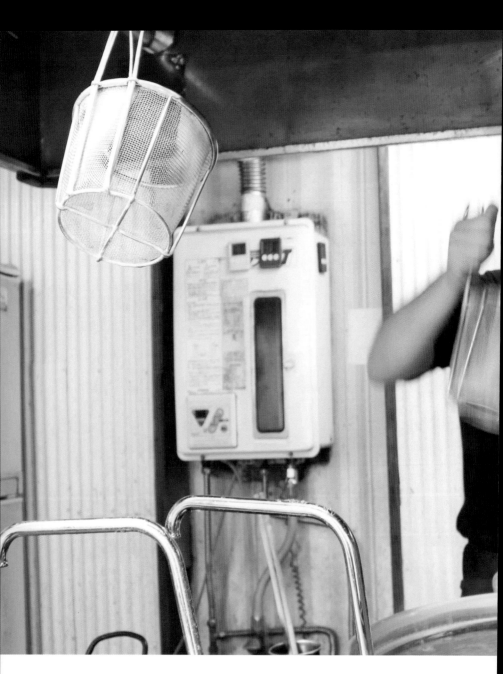

# Mentatsu

麺たつ

This famous shop is tucked away a bit of a distance from the JR Ōtsuka Station. The menu is mainly comprised of salt-based and soy sauce-based ramen. Ramen freaks give this establishment high marks, as each bowl prepared by the shop owner is made without compromise, with dedication to the finest details, such as in the thickness of the noodles to pair with the soup. The desire here is to have customers enjoy the ultimate bowl of ramen, where every single element - the noodles, soup, and toppings - is in perfect harmony.

159

# Recommend items

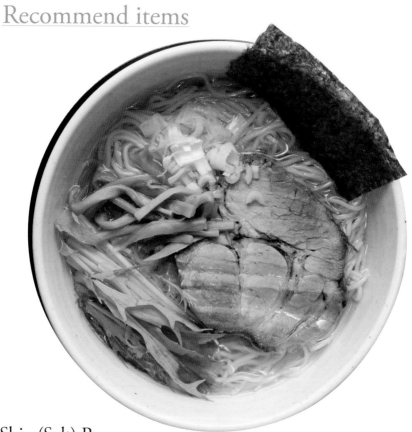

## Shio (Salt) Ramen

塩ラーメン

### 650JPY

This bowl is the culmination of extensive trial and error by the shop owner, finally arriving at the use of Okinawa salt. The soup, the beauty of which - sparkling like crystal - you will understand, simply looks delicious! The harmony created by the umami flavor of chicken and seafood extract is truly exquisite.

#### Noodles data

Noodle thickness: Medium fine
Noodle shape: Straight

#### Soup data

Rich☆☆☆☆★Light

Sauce: Salt
Oil: Chicken oil / Green onion oil
Type: Chicken chintan

# Shoyu (Soy Sauce) Ramen

正油ラーメン

## 630JPY

The secret to the delicious flavor of this soup lies in the original sauce, a blend of various ingredients, including dark soy sauce, white soy sauce, and charsiu sauce. The toppings have been whittled down to the most sparest of choices, a configuration of simplicity that indicates a thoughtfully careful dedication to detail.

### Noodles data

Noodle thickness: Medium thick
Noodle shape: Curly

### Soup data

Rich☆☆☆☆★Light

-------------------------------------------------

Sauce: Soy sauce
Oil: Chicken oil / Green onion oil
Type: Chicken chintan

メニュー

★
① 塩ラーメン（鶏油）　六五〇円
② 揚げネギ塩ラーメン　七〇〇円
★
③ 正油ラーメン（鶏油）　六三〇円
④ 揚げネギ正油ラーメン　六八〇円
⑤ 特麺たつ塩ラーメン　八九〇円
⑥ 特麺たつ正油ラーメン　八六〇円
⑦ 大盛り 一〇〇円増し

※注文の際に麺の固さや味加減等お申し付けください

トッピング
⑧ 味付け玉子 九〇円
⑨ のり 九〇円
⑩ メンマ 一一〇円
⑪ 白髪葱 一五〇円
⑫ チャーシュー 三一〇円

⑬ 餃子 三五〇円
⑭ チャーシュー丼 二五〇円
⑮ ビール 中ビン 五〇〇円
⑯ ウーロンハイ 三五〇円
⑰ ライス 一五〇円
⑱ 小ライス 一〇〇円

# Menu

There aren't many things on the menu, which makes me feel like they have confidence in their products.

| | |
|---|---|
| ❶ Salt Ramen 650JPY ★ | ❿ Menma (Fermented Bamboo Shoots) Topping 120JPY |
| ❷ Fried Green Onion Salt Ramen 700JPY | ⓫ Green Onion 150JPY |
| ❸ Soy Sauce Ramen 630JPY ★ | ⓬ Charsiu 320JPY |
| ❹ Fried Green Onion Soy sauce Ramen 680JPY | ⓭ Gyoza 350JPY |
| ❺ Special Mentatsu Salt Ramen 890JPY | ⓮ Charsiu Rice Bowl 250JPY |
| ❻ Special Mentatsu Soy Sauce Ramen 860JPY | ⓯ Bottled beer 500JPY |
| ❼ Large Serving (amount of noodles) 100JPY | ⓰ Oolong hai 350JPY |
| ❽ Marinated Egg Topping 90JPY | ⓱ Rice 150JPY |
| ❾ Dried seaweed Topping 90JPY | ⓲ Small rice 100JPY |

★ =Recommen items

# Order & Payment

01 Past the entrance is the counter, where you can seat yourself wherever available

02 Read the menu to find and order items you would like to eat

03 Order toppings together with your ramen

04 Customize noodle thickness and richness of flavor to taste

# Inside the shop

The interior is simply constructed, with only a counter.
Wait and watch the owner prepare your ramen.

Counter/9

餃子
三五〇円

おつまみに
メンマ 二二〇円
チャーシュー 三三〇円

メニュー

ウーロンハイ
三五〇円

Since this is a very popular shop, it will be better if
you avoid dinner time.

Chicken, seafood such as shellfish adductor muscles and kelp, and vegetables are simmered in low heat - without boiling - for 4 hours. Painstaking care to remove the coagulated foam buildup results in a clear soup.

## Shop keeper's Comment

For about 10 years I have trained in a variety of ramen shops. Through that experience I finally established my own flavor and opened up my own shop 8 years ago. Please come and visit, and enjoy a chicken-based ramen prepared with great care and effort.

## Shop Information

Address: 1-4-4, Nishisugamo, Toshima-ku, Tokyo

Open: 5:00pm-12:00am

Closed on Wednesdays

# Papapapapine

パパパパパイン

As you can tell by the name of the shop, the ramen here, to our surprise, uses pineapple. This unexpected innovation brought the shop a large amount of attention ever since its opening. And as to the taste... to our surprise, it's actually delicious. The acidity and sweetness of the pineapple actually matches perfectly with the simplicity of the salt-based soup. Here, you can experience mouthwatering flavors unlike anything you've ever had before.

# Recommend items

## Pineapple Salt Ramen with Marinated Egg

パイナップル塩ラーメン＋味玉

### 720JPY+100JPY

The distinction of this Pineapple Ramen is that no animal products whatsoever have been used, instead featuring a soup stock extracted from Japanese style niboshi, kombu, and shiitake mushrooms, blended with pineapple fruit juices. The citric acidity of the pineapple matches well with the umami flavor of the soup.

#### Noodles data

Noodle thickness: Fine
Noodle shape: Straight

#### Soup data

Rich☆☆☆☆★Light

--------------------------------------------------

Sauce: Salt
Oil: Green onion oil
Type: Seafood

170

## Noodles data

Noodle thickness: Fine
Noodle shape: Straight

## Soup data

Rich ☆☆☆☆★ Light

- - - - - - - - - - - - - - - - - - - - - - - - - - - -

Sauce: Salt
Oil: Green onion oil
Type: Seafood

# Pineapple Salt Dipping Noodles

パイナップル塩つけめん

## 770JPY

Where other shops may use sugar or vinegar in their soup, this shop uses pineapple fruit juices instead. The natural sweetness and acidity come out in the flavors, and result in an extremely well-balanced taste.

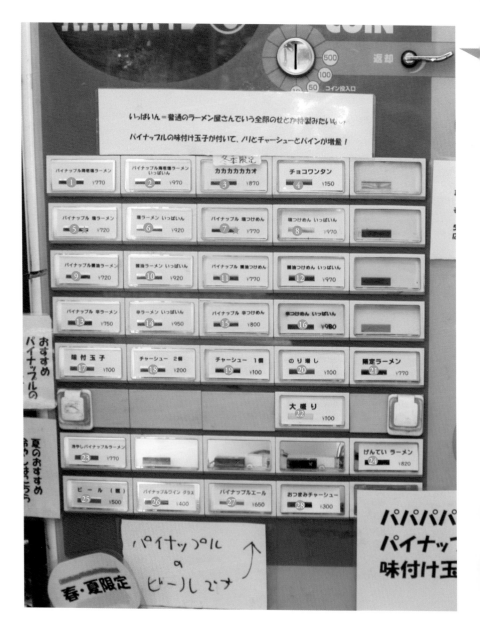

# Menu

Every item on the menu uses pineapple.

That dedication extends even to the wine and beer.

- ❶ Pineapple Shrimp Salt Ramen 770JPY
- ❷ Pineapple Shrimp Salt Ramen(All toppings) 970JPY
- ❸ Ca Ca Ca Ca Cacao(Winter limited) 870JPY
- ❹ Chocolate Won-ton 150JPY
- ❺ Pineapple Salt Ramen 720JPY ★
- ❻ Pineapple Salt Ramen(All toppings) 920JPY
- ❼ Pineapple Salt Dipping Noodles 770JPY ★
- ❽ Pineapple Salt Dipping Noodles(All toppings) 970JPY
- ❾ Pineapple Soy Sauce Ramen 720JPY
- ❿ Pineapple Soy Sauce Ramen(All toppings) 920JPY
- ⑪ Pineapple Soy Sauce Dipping Noodles 770JPY
- ⑫ Pineapple Soy Sauce Dipping Noodles(All toppings) 970JPY
- ⑬ Pineapple Spicy Ramen 750JPY
- ⑭ Pineapple Spicy Ramen(All toppings) 950JPY

- ⑮ Pineapple Spicy Dipping Noodles 800JPY
- ⑯ Pineapple Spicy Dipping Noodles(All toppings) 980JPY
- ⑰ Marinated Egg Topping 100JPY
- ⑱ Charsiu Topping(2p) 200JPY
- ⑲ Charsiu Topping(1p) 100JPY
- ⑳ Dried seaweed Topping 100JPY
- ㉑ Limited Ramen#1 770JPY
- ㉒ Large Serving (amount of noodles) 100JPY
- ㉓ Cold Pineapple Ramen 770JPY
- ㉔ Limited Ramen#2 820JPY
- ㉕ Bottle Beer 500JPY
- ㉖ Pineapple Wine 400JPY
- ㉗ Pineapple Beer 650JPY
- ㉘ Charsiu 300JPY

★=Recommen items

# Order & Payment

01 There is a ticket machine outside, where you insert money and press the button to choose your meal items

02 Sit at an available seat, and a staff member will bring you water

03 Hand your ticket to the staff member

# Inside the shop

The interior of the shop is filled with pineapple-themed decorations.
The scent of ramen and pineapples stimulate your tastebuds.

Counter/12

Garlic toppings are provided for free. If you would
like some, please ask for it when ordering.

1/4 of the soup is made up of pineapple fruit juices. Even the charsiu pork toppings are made with pineapple fruit juices.

## Shop keeper's Comment

After training at a famous ramen shop in Takadanobaba, I decided to open up a ramen shop unlike any other, and so I decided to take on the challenge of making ramen using pineapples. Currently I am also trying out an assortment of limited edition menu items. I hope you will come visit and try our pineapple ramen.

## Shop Information

Address:3-12-1, Nishiogiminami, Suginami-ku, Tokyo

Open:11:00am-11:00pm(Mon-Fri), 11:00am-8:00pm(Sat,Sun)

Open 7days

# Ramen Zundo-Ya
## Shinjuku Shop

ラー麺 ずんどう屋 新宿店

Established in Himeji, in Hyogo Prefecture. With its deep and rich tonkotsu ramen garnering wide acclaim, the shop quickly became famous in the Kansai region, and eventually led to its first Kanto store opening in Shinjuku. With a determined dedication to quality in all ingredients, the ramen prepared here has gained a wide following among many people. The richness of the soup, and the different types of noodles are all qualities that can happily be appreciated in all their fine detail.

# Ajitama(Marinated egg) Ramen

味玉ラーメン

## 890JPY

After carefully preparing choice pork bone, it is slowly simmered for about 20 hours to produce a deliciously concentrated, creamy soup. Although rich in flavor, it has a refreshingly simple aftertaste. The amount of back fat can be selected from 4 different quantity stages to allow a customized taste.

Noodles data

Noodle thickness: Fine
Noodle shape: Straight

Soup data

Rich ★☆☆☆☆ Light
----------------------------------
Sauce: Soy sauce
Oil: Back fat
Type: Tonkotsu

# Kabuki Set
# (Regular size serving)

歌舞伎セット（並）

### 440JPY

With a large lineup of side dishes, one of the most popular is this set. Featuring gyoza and karaage chicken together, it feels like a bonus. There is also a large size serving with more pieces of each item added.

# Menu

Distinct for its large variety of available side dishes. And all items are superb dishes that go great with beer & sake.

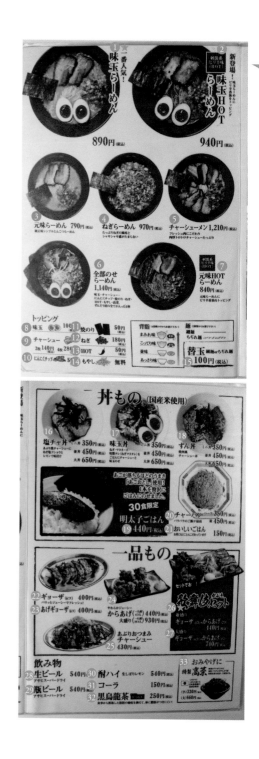

- ❶ Ramen with Marinated Egg 890JPY ★
- ❷ Spicy Ramen with Marinated Egg 940JPY
- ❸ Ramen 790JPY
- ❹ Ramen with Green Onion 970JPY
- ❺ Charsiu Ramen 1210JPY
- ❻ All toppings Ramen 1140JPY
- ❼ Spicy Ramen 840JPY
- ❽ Marinated Egg Topping100JPY
- ❾ Charsiu Topping(2p)140JPY,(4p)280JPY
- ❿ Garlic Chips Topping 50JPY
- ⓫ Dried seaweed Topping 50JPY
- ⓬ Green Onion Topping 180JPY
- ⓭ Spices Topping 50JPY
- ⓮ Sprout Topping Free
- ⓯ Kaedama (Second serving of noodles) 100JPY
- ⓰ Salt Charsiu Rice Bowl (S)350JPY,(M)450JPY,(L)650JPY
- ⓱ Marinated Egg Rice Bowl (S)350JPY,(M)450JPY,(L)650JPY

- ⓲ Zundo-ya's Rice Bowl (S)350JPY,(M)450JPY,(L)650JPY
- ⓳ Seasoned cod roe Rice Bowl 440JPY
- ⓴ Fried rice (Half size)350JPY,(Regular size)450JPY
- ㉑ Rice 150JPY
- ㉒ Gyoza 400JPY
- ㉓ Fried Gyoza 400JPY
- ㉔ Fried Chicken(4p)440JPY,(10p)930JPY
- ㉕ Broiled Charsiu 430JPY
- ㉖ Kabuki Set/Regular size serving 440JPY ★
- ㉗ Kabuki Set/Large size serving 740JPY
- ㉘ Draft Beer 540JPY
- ㉙ Bottle Beer 540JPY
- ㉚ Chuhai (Shochu High-Ball) with Freshly-Squeezed Lemon 540JPY
- ㉛ Coca Cola 150JPY
- ㉜ Black Oolong Tea 250JPY
- ㉝ Speciality Pickled Mustard (S)330JPY,(L)660JPY ※ gift set product)

★=Recommen items

# Order & Payment

01 Come through the entrance, and sit at an available seat

02 Look over the menu to find a dish you'd like to eat

03 A staff member will bring you water

04 Place your order with the staff member. You can choose the strength of flavor

05 Feel free to use the raw garlic and other seasonings available on the counter. Season to taste!

# Inside the shop

A rather large interior. Distinctive for its many tables with room to seat large groups. How about eating some ramen while gazing at the comings and goings in Kabukicho?

Table seat/31    Counter/8

Use the raw garlic and other seasonings available on the counter to season your food to taste.

A large kitchen, designed to prepare orders quickly. It's uncommon to see a karaage deep frying machine installed to prepare this popular side dish.

## Shop keeper's Comment

We designed this shop so that customers from overseas can enjoy themselves here. We have used a large amount of wood furnishings to create a warm and comfortable atmosphere. We have absolute confidence in our pride and joy, the "Deep and Rich Tonkotsu Ramen," so please come by and enjoy a bowl.

## Shop Information

Address: 2-39-3, Kabukicho, Shinjuku-ku, Tokyo

Open: 24/7

※Closed for maintenance from 6:00 am to 11:00am after the close of late night business on Sunday and the last day of consecutive holidays.

# Menya CoCoichi
## Akihabara Shop

麺屋ここいち 秋葉原店

It's been 10 years since the super popular curry house CoCo ICHIBANYA began developing ramen dishes, based on their curry recipes. Little by little, they revised the form and style until they completed their curry ramen. Just like the curry house CoCo ICHIBANYA, you can customize the serving size, spiciness, and toppings, so you can discover a curry ramen to fit your tastes.

# Recommend items

## Deep and Rich
## Delicious Curry Ramen

濃厚うまこくカレーらーめん

### 810JPY

The soup is prepared by extracting the essence of pork and chicken bones and combining with more than 20 different spices to create a superb mix of hot spiciness, together with the thick umami of simmered vegetables, concentrated into a delicious fusion of flavors. This is the ultimate bowl of ramen, crafted by a curry specialty shop.

### Noodles data

Noodle thickness: Thick
Noodle shape: Straight

### Soup data

Rich ★☆☆☆☆ Light

Sauce: Curry
Oil: Back fat
Type: Curry, tonkotsu, torigara

# Sauce-Dipped Cutlet Curry Ramen

タレカツカレーらーめん

### 813JPY

Based on the curry spices that are beloved at CoCo ICHIBANYA, a unique blend of flavors have been prepared to create this rich and tasty soup. Delicious on its own, but when dipped in the raw egg included in the set meal, the umami is enhanced even more.

<u>Noodles data</u>

Noodle thickness: Medium thick
Noodle shape: Straight

<u>Soup data</u>

Rich☆☆★☆☆Light

- - - - - - - - - - - - - - - - - - - - - - - - - - - - - - - - -

Sauce: Curry
Oil: Back fat
Type: Secret

# Menu

The menu features mainly curry items, but has been expanded to include a wide range of food, including rice dishes.

| | | | |
|---|---|---|---|
| ① Rich Delicious Curry Ramen 702JPY | | ⑲ Extra Meat Topping 205JPY | |
| ② Deep and Rich Delicious Curry Ramen 810JPY | ★ | ⑳ Ripe tomatoes Topping 206JPY | |
| ③ Charsiu Curry Ramen 1058JPY | | ㉑ Charsiu Topping 216JPY | |
| ④ Big-Appetite Curry Ramen 1058JPY | | ㉒ Innards Stew Pork Topping 258JPY | |
| ⑤ Curry Ramen with Cheese 810JPY | | ㉓ Gyoza,Fried Gyoza Topping 259JPY | |
| ⑥ Curry Ramen with Cutlet 939JPY | | ㉔ Cutlet Topping 464JPY | |
| ⑦ Sauce-Dipped Cutlet Curry Ramen 813JPY | ★ | ㉕ Rice (S)86JPY, (M)172JPY,(L)248JPY | |
| ⑧ Curry Ramen with Tomato&Cheese 1016JPY | | ㉖ Fried rice/Half size 291JPY | |
| ⑨ Curry Ramen with Marinated Egg 810JPY | | ㉗ Fried rice 594JPY | |
| ⑩ Curry Ramen with Iwanori 1095JPY | | ㉘ Rice(into the bowl) 43JPY | |
| ⑪ Meat Curry Soba 907JPY | | ㉙ Sauce-Dipped Cutlet Rice Bowl 516JPY | |
| ⑫ Curry Ramen with Gyoza 913JPY | | ㉚ Sauce-Dipped Cutlet Rice Bowl/Small Size 258JPY | |
| ⑬ Spicy Miso Curry Ramen 868JPY | | ㉛ Innards Stew Pork Rice Bowl/Small Size 361JPY | |
| ⑭ Curry Ramen with Dried seaweed &Butter&Corn 972JPY | | ㉜ Innards Stew Pork 258JPY | |
| ⑮ Boiled Sprout,Boiled Cabbage,Chopped Green Onion,Raw egg,Rich Taste/Toppings 54JPY | | ㉝ Gyoza 259JPY | |
| | | ㉞ Fried Gyoza 259JPY | |
| ⑯ Meat miso,Marinated Egg,Corn,Butter,Cheese,Iwanori/Toppings 108JPY | | ㉟ Beer 324JPY | |
| | | ㊱ Kirin Mets Cola 248JPY | |
| ⑰ Sauce-Dipped Cutlet Topping 139JPY | | ㊲ Karada Sukoyaka Tea 248JPY | |
| ⑱ Spinach,Spicy Miso Topping 151JPY | | | |

★=Recommen items

# Order & Payment

01 Enter, and sit at an available seat

02 Water is self-service, so pour yourself a drink!

03 Place your order with a staff member

04 The pickled vegetables available on the counter are free of charge

# Inside the shop

Seating is available only at the counter. Menus and water are organized in evenly placed intervals on the counter top.

Counter/10

Pickled vegetables and spices to make your food hotter are available on the counter and free to use.

From the counter you can see the kitchen, where the staff skillfully mixes a meat-based soup and curry sauce to prepare the curry ramen. The many different spices are the deciding factor, after all.

## Shop keeper's Comment

After running CoCo ICHI-BANYA (curry) shops in Niigata, Tokyo, Saitama, and Ibaraki, I decided to join their new ramen venture and it's been 3 years now. I will continue to proudly serve bowls of delicious curry and ramen.

## Shop Information

Address:16, Kandamatsunagacho, Chiyoda-ku, Tokyo

Open:11:00am-11:00pm(Mon-Thu,Sat), 11:00am-12:00pm(Fri), 11:00am-9:00 pm(Sun)

Open 7days

# Welcome

Finally, we'll introduce a ramen restaurant in Haneda Airport
where you can eat just after you've arrived in Japan.

# to japan.

# Setagaya
## Haneda International Airport Shop

せたが屋　羽田国際空港店

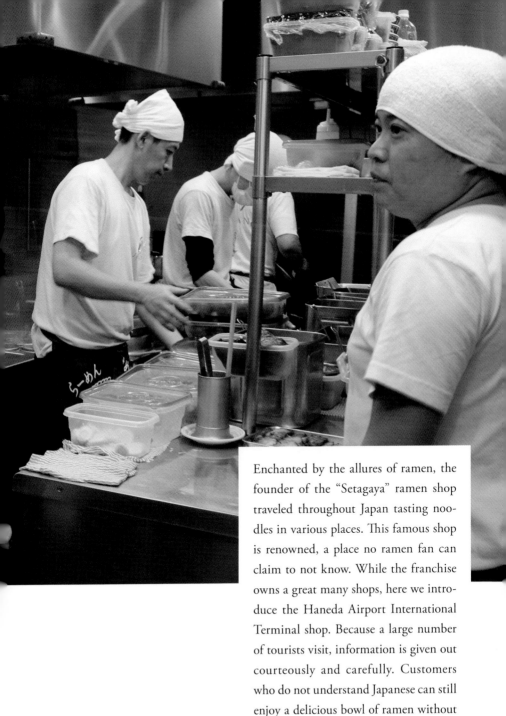

Enchanted by the allures of ramen, the founder of the "Setagaya" ramen shop traveled throughout Japan tasting noodles in various places. This famous shop is renowned, a place no ramen fan can claim to not know. While the franchise owns a great many shops, here we introduce the Haneda Airport International Terminal shop. Because a large number of tourists visit, information is given out courteously and carefully. Customers who do not understand Japanese can still enjoy a delicious bowl of ramen without any confusion or problems.

# Recommend items

## Setagaya Ramen

せたが屋らーめん

### 1080JPY

The soup is a slowly simmered mixture of pork and chicken bones. With an added accent of dried sardines and dried bonito, a deeply rich meaty flavoring and seafood fragrance expands inside the mouth. The medium thick curly noodles are chewy with a delicious texture. This is a popular item that represents this shop well.

#### Noodles data

Noodle thickness: Medium thick
Noodle shape: Curly

#### Soup data

Rich☆★☆☆☆Light

----------------------------------------

Sauce: Soy sauce
Oil: Secret
Type: Tonkotsu and seafood

# Tonkotsu
# Ramen
# with all toppings

とんこつらーめん

**1030JPY**

In order to remove the distinct smell that tonkotsu ramen has, ginger, garlic, and green onions are used. For that reason the tonkotsu soup here is less viscous than at other shops, and results in a flavor that is easy for first-time tonkotsu diners to enjoy.

Noodles data

Noodle thickness: Ultra fine
Noodle shape: Straight

Soup data

Rich☆☆☆★☆Light

----------------------------------------

Sauce: Soy sauce, miso, salt
Oil: None used
Type: Tonkotsu

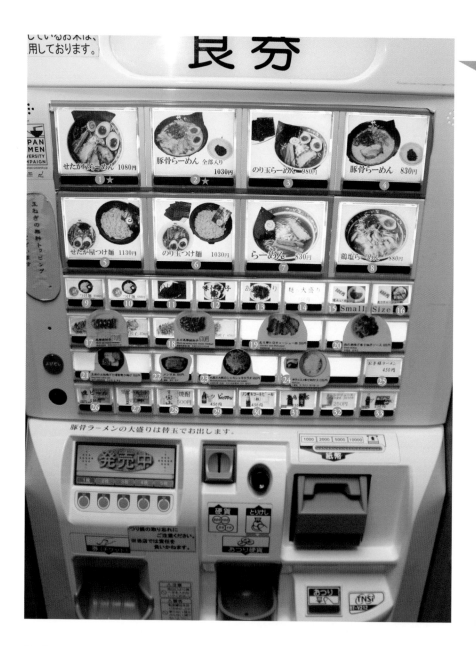

# Menu

Happily, the menu offers not only ramen,
but a wide selection of side dishes and even sake.

| | | | |
|---|---|---|---|
| ① Setagaya Ramen 1080JPY ★ | | ⑱ Black Pork Green Onion Gyoza 670JPY |
| ② Tonkotsu Ramen(All toppings) 1030JPY ★ | | ⑲ Broiled Charsiu Dish 500JPY |
| ③ Ramen with Marinated Egg&Seaweed 980JPY | | ⑳ Fried Chicken Citron flavor 600JPY |
| ④ Tonkotsu Ramen 830JPY | | ㉑ Tofu and Seaweed Rolled Fried 550JPY |
| ⑤ Setagaya Dipping Noodles 1130JPY | | ㉒ Menma (Fermented Bamboo Shoots) Dish 300JPY |
| ⑥ Setagaya Dipping Noodles with Marinated Egg&Seaweed 1030JPY | | ㉓ Mizuna and Radish Salad 450JPY |
| | | ㉔ Small Rice with pickles 200JPY |
| ⑦ Ramen 830JPY | | ㉕ Kids'Ramen 450JPY |
| ⑧ Chicken Salt Ramen 880JPY | | ㉖ Draft Beer 510JPY |
| ⑨ Dipping Noodles 880JPY | | ㉗ Draft Beer/Small size 350JPY |
| ⑩ Dipping Noodles( ⑨ Same menu) 880JPY | | ㉘ Shochu 500JPY |
| ⑪ Dried seaweed Topping 100JPY | | ㉙ Hoppy Set 450JPY |
| ⑫ Marinated Egg Topping 150JPY | | ㉚ Non-alcoholic Beer 450JPY |
| ⑬ Sea Lettuce Topping 150JPY | | ㉛ Black Oolong Tea 350JPY |
| ⑭ Large Serving (amount of noodles) 150JPY | | ㉜ Orange Juice 250JPY |
| ⑮ Curry Rice/Small size 500JPY | | ㉝ Pepsi-Cola 250JPY |
| ⑯ Broiled Charsiu Rice Bowl/Small size 400JPY | | |
| ⑰ Black Pork Gyoza 570JPY | | |

★=Recommen items

# Order & Payment

01 At the front of the entrance is a ticket machine, where you insert money and press the button to choose your meal items

02 Sit at an available seat and hand your ticket to a staff member

03 Water is self-service, so pour yourself a drink!

04 The seasonings available on the counter are free to use. So season to taste!

# Inside the shop

Wood furnishings lend a comfortable air to the interiors. The menus are written in easily understandable English, Chinese, and Korean languages.

Table seat/12    Counter/8

On the counter are dispensers of "Gatsun juice"(Impact juice) that, when added to your soup, will make the flavor deeper and stronger.

This is ramen made with a dedication to fine ingredients. Happily, with a large number of staff on hand, you won't wait long for your ramen to be delivered after placing your order.

## Shop keeper's Comment

For first time visitors, we recommend the seafood-based "Setagaya Ramen." The "Tonkotsu" is also very popular with foreign guests. For diners who like their food spicy, the spicy miso called "Ra-jan" is added to the soup and is highly acclaimed. We hope you will come by and enjoy our range of different flavors.

## Shop Information

Address:2-6-5, Hanedakuko, Ota-ku, Tokyo

Open:5:00am-12:00am(Mon-Sun)

Open 7days

So have a

# good trip!

PRESENTS

# TOKYO RAMEN

## Perfect Guide Book

Publisher:Suniwa CO,LTD
4-28-8-601, Yoyogi,Shibuya-ku,Tokyo,Japan

Design:Hoshi Design Station(www.hoshi.st)

···yes! web site
http://japan-ramen.com/

Facebook
https://www.facebook.com/tokyo.ramen.mag

Instagram
https://www.instagram.com/japan_ramen_mag/

info
info@suniwa.com

※The pricing and menu information on this publication is current as of October 10th 2015. Please note that the menu may differ depending on the shop. Thank you for your understanding.

PRESENTS

# 東京ラーメン

パーフェクト ガイド ブック

2016年3月10日　初版第1刷発行

企画・制作：株式会社Suniwa
〒151-0053東京都渋谷区代々木4-28-8-601
電話：03-6276-1157

発行者：柳卓也

発行・発売所：日販アイ・ピー・エス株式会社
〒113-0034東京都文京区湯島1-3-4
電話：03-5802-1859

装丁デザイン協力：Hoshi Design Station

印刷・製本：凸版印刷株式会社